DEEP LEARNING FOR CREATIVE AI

DR. A. SATHIYARAJ

Made with ♥ on the Notion Press Platform
www.notionpress.com

Contents

CHAPTER ONE

Introduction

Deep learning is a subfield of machine learning that has revolutionized artificial intelligence in recent years. Its ability to tackle complex tasks involving pattern recognition and prediction has made it the driving force behind breakthroughs in various domains, from self-driving cars to medical diagnosis. But what exactly is this magic under the hood? Let's dive into the details:

1. Inspiration from the Brain

At its core, deep learning is inspired by the structure and function of the human brain. It utilizes artificial neural networks, which are computational models mimicking the interconnected network of neurons in our brains. These networks consist of multiple layers of processing units called neurons that communicate with each other and learn from data.

The inspiration from the brain is fundamental to understanding deep learning. Let's break down the key aspects of this inspiration:

1. Structure of the Brain: Imagine your brain as a vast network of interconnected cells called neurons. These neurons communicate with each other by sending electrical signals through axons and receiving inputs through dendrites. This interconnectedness allows the brain to learn and process information in a distributed and parallel manner.

2. Artificial Neural Networks: Deep learning models mimic this interconnected structure of the brain by using artificial neurons. These are computational units that receive inputs from previous layers, perform calculations using an activation function, and send

outputs to subsequent layers. This creates a multi-layered network that can process information progressively, extracting increasingly complex features as it goes.

3. Layers of Processing: Unlike simpler neural networks, deep learning models have multiple hidden layers between the input and output layers. Each layer focuses on extracting specific features from the data. For example, in image recognition, the first layers might detect edges and color gradients, while higher layers might assemble these features to recognize objects like faces or buildings.

4. Communication and Learning: Just like neurons in the brain, artificial neurons "talk" to each other by sending weighted signals across connections. These weights determine how much influence each neuron has on the next layer. Through a process called backpropagation, the network adjusts these weights based on how well it performs on training data. Imagine it as correcting its mistakes step-by-step to improve its understanding of the problem.

5. Advantages of this Brain-Inspired Design: This brain-inspired architecture gives deep learning several advantages:

- Non-linearity: Activation functions introduce non-linearity into the network, allowing it to capture complex relationships in data that linear models can't.
- Hierarchical Feature Extraction: Each layer extracts progressively more complex features, building a layered representation of the data.
- Parallel Processing: Multiple layers can process information simultaneously, leading to faster and more efficient learning.

Although deep learning models are inspired by the brain, they are still significantly simpler and computationally different. The brain operates on vastly more complex principles, involving billions of neurons with intricate connections and biophysical processes not yet fully understood.

2. Architecture of Deep Learning:

Layers: Unlike simpler neural networks, deep learning models have multiple hidden layers between the input and output layers. These layers extract increasingly complex features from the data as it flows through the network. Imagine each layer as a filter refining the information for the next layer. Activation functions are the unsung heroes of deep learning, playing a crucial role in transforming linear neurons into powerful pattern-extracting machines. Think of them as gates that control the flow of information through the network, adding crucial non-linearity that allows the model to learn complex relationships in data.

Here's how activation functions work their magic:

1. Breaking the Linearity Barrier: Without activation functions, deep learning networks would be just fancy glorified calculators. They would only be able to learn relationships that can be represented by straight lines (linear functions). This severely limits their ability to capture the intricate patterns and non-linear dependencies that exist in real-world data.

2. Introducing the Curve: Activation functions come in various shapes and sizes, each introducing a unique non-linearity to the network. For example, the popular sigmoid function squashes its output between 0 and 1, mimicking the firing rate of a biological neuron. Imagine it as a gentle S-shaped curve that transforms incoming signals into a range suitable for further processing.

3. Why Non-linearity Matters: This seemingly simple trick unlocks a world of possibilities. By introducing non-linearity, activation functions enable the network to:

- Learn complex decision boundaries: Instead of just drawing straight lines, the network can now learn decision boundaries with curves and bends, allowing it to accurately separate different classes of data.
- Build hierarchical representations: Each layer with an activation function can extract increasingly complex features from the data. Imagine stacking these layers like building blocks, with each layer adding a new level of abstraction and meaning.

- Encode context and relationships: Non-linearity allows the network to capture subtle relationships between different parts of the data, not just isolated features. This context makes it possible for the model to understand the bigger picture and perform tasks like predicting future values in a sequence or recognizing objects in an image.

4. Choosing the Right Function: Different activation functions have their own strengths and weaknesses. Choosing the right one for your model depends on factors like the type of data, the network architecture, and the desired outcome. Some popular options include:

- Sigmoid: Good for binary classification tasks.
- Tanh: Similar to sigmoid, but centered around zero.
- ReLU (Rectified Linear Unit): Fast and efficient, widely used for its simplicity and lack of vanishing gradients.
- Leaky ReLU: A variant of ReLU that allows small negative values, mitigating the "dying ReLU" problem.

Understanding activation functions is essential for navigating the intricate world of deep learning. They serve as the backbone of non-linearity, providing the network with the tools it needs to unravel complex patterns and unlock true learning potential.

Activation Functions: These functions introduce non-linearity into the network, allowing it to capture complex relationships in the data and avoid the limitations of simpler linear models. Activation functions are the key to unlocking the true power of deep learning by adding that crucial spark of non-linearity. Here are some additional points to expand on how they achieve this:

1. Beyond Straight Lines: Imagine a simple linear model. It can only learn relationships that can be represented by straight lines. This means data points can only be separated by hyperplanes, which is pretty limiting for real-world data that often has complex, non-linear patterns.

2. Bending the Rules: That's where activation functions come in. They introduce curves and bends into the model's response, allowing it to learn complex decision boundaries that traditional linear models cannot. It's like adding a secret weapon to the network's arsenal, enabling it to handle intricate relationships between data points.

3. Building Blocks of Complexity: Think of each layer with an activation function as a building block. They stack on top of each other, taking the transformed input from the previous layer and introducing another layer of non-linearity. This allows the network to build increasingly complex feature representations, capturing subtle relationships and context within the data.

4. From Pixels to Objects: For example, in image recognition, the first layers might extract basic features like edges and color gradients. Later layers, fueled by activation functions, can combine these features and learn to recognize shapes, textures, and ultimately, objects like faces or cars. This wouldn't be possible without the non-linear transformations happening behind the scenes.

5. More Than Just Classification: While non-linearity is crucial for tasks like classification, it also powers other deep learning applications. For example, in sequence prediction, activation functions allow the network to capture temporal dependencies between elements, predicting future values based on the context of the past.

6. Beyond the S-Curve: Don't be fooled by the popular sigmoid function, which is just one example of non-linearity. Researchers are constantly exploring new activation functions with different properties, each suitable for specific tasks and network architectures. The possibilities are endless!

To summarize, activation functions are the hidden heroes of deep learning, breathing life into the network by introducing the magic of non-linearity. They empower the model to go beyond straight lines, capture complex relationships, and unlock the true potential of deep learning for tackling a wide range of real-world challenges.

Learning Process: Through a method called backpropagation, the network adjusts the weights and connections between neurons based on how well it performs on training data. It's like continuously correcting its mistakes to improve its understanding of the problem.Backpropagation is indeed like a tireless teacher constantly guiding the deep learning network to improve its performance. Let's delve deeper into this fascinating learning process:

1. The Quest for Minimizing Error: Imagine the network is presented with training data (think of it as examples with desired outputs). It makes its initial predictions based on its current set of weights and connections between neurons. However, these predictions are rarely perfect, resulting in an error between the network's output and the desired output.

2. Backtracking the Mistake: This is where backpropagation comes in. It starts with the error at the output layer and calculates how much each neuron in the previous layer contributed to that error. This is done by applying the chain rule of differentiation, essentially backtracking the path the error took through the network.

3. Adjusting the Weights: Imagine each weight as a knob that controls the influence of one neuron on another. Backpropagation calculates how much to adjust each of these knobs based on their contribution to the error. Smaller adjustments are made for neurons with less influence, while larger adjustments are made for those with a bigger impact.

4. Gradient Descent: This process of calculating and applying weight adjustments is known as gradient descent. Think of it as rolling a ball down a hill (the error function) towards the valley (minimum error). Each backpropagation step is like a small nudge, guiding the network closer to the optimal set of weights that minimize the overall error.

5. Continuous Learning: The beauty of backpropagation is its iterative nature. The network repeatedly goes through this process

of prediction, error calculation, and weight adjustment, with each iteration refining its understanding of the problem. It's like learning through trial and error, constantly improving its predictions based on feedback from the training data.

6. Analogy of a Student: Imagine a student practicing for a test. Each attempt is a prediction, and the grade is the error signal. Backpropagation acts like a dedicated tutor, identifying the mistakes in each answer and providing detailed feedback (weight adjustments) to help the student improve for the next try.

7. The Power of Optimization: Through this continuous learning process, deep learning networks can eventually achieve remarkable levels of accuracy and performance. Backpropagation helps them optimize their internal structure, allowing them to find complex patterns and relationships in the data.

Backpropagation is a powerful tool, but it can be computationally expensive for large networks and complex datasets. Ongoing research is focused on optimizing and speeding up the process to make deep learning even more accessible and powerful.

3. Types of Deep Learning Models:

Convolutional Neural Networks (CNNs)

Masterminds behind image recognition and computer vision, CNNs excel at processing grid-like data like images and videos. They use filters to extract specific features like edges and textures, building a representation of the whole image step-by-step.

Convolutional Neural Networks (CNNs) are the rockstars of image recognition and computer vision, and their ability to dissect and understand visual data is truly remarkable. Let's dive deeper into how they manage this feat:

1. Grid Champions: Unlike standard neural networks that treat data as flat vectors, CNNs excel at processing grid-like structures like images and videos. They understand that spatial relationships within the data are crucial for tasks like recognizing objects or identifying scenes.

2. Feature Extraction Champs: The magic of CNNs lies in their filters. These are small matrices that slide across the input image, detecting specific features like edges, textures, or colors. Imagine them as tiny detectives searching for clues within the visual grid.

3. Feature Maps Revealed:As the filter scans the image, it produces a "feature map" highlighting the detected feature's presence and strength at each location. Stacking multiple filters leads to multiple feature maps, each capturing a different aspect of the image, like horizontal lines, corners, or specific textures.

4. Hierarchical Understanding: The real power lies in the layered architecture of CNNs. Each layer of filters builds upon the previous one, extracting increasingly complex features. Imagine starting with edges and textures, then combining them to detect shapes and patterns, and eventually recognizing entire objects like faces or cars.

5. Pooling for Efficiency: To avoid drowning in too much detail, CNNs use pooling layers. These downsample the feature maps, reducing their size while retaining the most important information. Think of it as summarizing the key findings from each detective's report before moving on to the next layer.

6. Connecting the Dots: Finally, the higher layers of the CNN take these complex feature maps and learn to combine them into a meaningful representation of the entire image. This final output can be used for various tasks, like classifying the image content, predicting what's happening in a video, or even generating new images based on the learned features.

7. Beyond Images:While CNNs shine in image-related tasks, their power extends beyond pixels. They can be adapted to process other grid-like data, like audio spectrograms or even text data represented as matrices. This makes them incredibly versatile tools for various applications.

Remember: CNNs are complex mechanisms, and understanding them fully requires exploring mathematical details and specific architectures. However, this broad overview hopefully gives you a grasp of their core principles and why they revolutionized the world of image recognition and computer vision.

Recurrent Neural Networks (RNNs): These networks are adept at handling sequential data like text and speech. They process information one element at a time, maintaining an internal memory of previous elements to understand the context. LSTM (Long Short-Term Memory) networks are a popular type of RNNs that can handle long sequences effectively.

Recurrent Neural Networks (RNNs) shine when it comes to sequential information like text and speech. Let's zoom in on how they handle this unique data type:

1. The Sequential Symphony: Unlike CNNs that process data in parallel, RNNs tackle information one element at a time. Imagine reading a sentence word by word, or listening to a speech sound by sound. Each element builds upon the previous ones, creating a context that's crucial for understanding the overall meaning.

2. Internal Memory of Past: This is where RNNs' hidden magic lies. They maintain an internal state or memory that captures information from previous elements in the sequence. Think of it as a running summary of what you've seen or heard so far, influencing how you interpret the next bit of information.

3. Unfolding the Network: RNNs have a unique architecture that unfolds over time. Imagine stacking several "copies" of the same basic neural network on top of each other, with each layer receiving information from the previous one and the input at that particular time step. This creates a chain of interconnected modules, each building upon the context established by its predecessors.

4. Vanishing Gradients: However, this sequential nature can pose a challenge. As information travels through the network, the gradients used for backpropagation can fade away, making it difficult to learn long-term dependencies. This is where LSTM networks come in.

5. Long Short-Term Memory (LSTM):LSTMs are a special type of RNN designed to combat vanishing gradients. They incorporate additional gates and memory cells that allow them to store and access information for longer periods. Imagine them as more

sophisticated note-takers, keeping track of important details from earlier parts of the sequence.

6. Applications Galore: With their ability to handle context and long sequences, RNNs excel in various tasks:

- Language modeling: Predicting the next word in a sentence, generating text, or translating languages.
- Speech recognition: Transcribing spoken words into text.
- Music generation: Creating new music pieces based on existing patterns.
- Stock price prediction: Analyzing historical data to forecast future market trends.

7. Challenges and Advancements: RNNs are still evolving, and researchers are exploring ways to improve their efficiency, handle very long sequences, and interpret their internal states for better explainability.

The world of RNNs is intricate and fascinating, with plenty of exciting research happening. This overview hopefully gives you a good grasp of their basic principles and highlights their potential in various real-world applications.

Generative Adversarial Networks (GANs): These involve two competing networks - a generator that creates new data (like images or music) and a discriminator that tries to distinguish it from real data. Through their adversarial interplay, the generator progressively improves its ability to create realistic and compelling outputs.

Generative Adversarial Networks (GANs) are like an artistic sparring match between two neural networks, pushing each other to new heights of creativity and realism. Let's dive into this fascinating dance of creation and critique:

1. Dueling Artists: Imagine two artists locked in a competition. One, the generator, strives to create ever-more convincing works of art, like paintings, images, or even music. The other, the discriminator, acts as a ruthless critic, trying to distinguish the

generator's creations from genuine real-world examples.

2. Learning Through Competition: This adversarial interplay is the heart of GANs. As the generator produces new outputs, the discriminator continuously refines its ability to tell real from fake. This feedback loop pushes the generator to improve its techniques, crafting increasingly realistic and compelling outputs to fool the ever-sharpening critic.

3. The Generator's Toolbox: Just like any artist, the generator has its own tools and tricks. It might utilize deep learning techniques like convolution and upsampling to manipulate noise or existing data, gradually shaping it into the desired form. The specific methods depend on the type of data being generated, from images and music to text and even 3D models.

4. The Discriminator's Scrutiny: Meanwhile, the discriminator doesn't sit idle. It analyzes the generated data using its own neural network architecture, searching for subtle telltale signs that reveal its artificial origin. This could involve identifying statistical inconsistencies, unrealistic textures, or even stylistic flaws that deviate from natural examples.

5. Continuous Refining: As the duel progresses, both networks constantly evolve. The generator learns from the discriminator's critiques, tweaking its approach to produce more convincing outputs. The discriminator, in turn, adapts to the generator's improvements, sharpening its detection skills to stay ahead of the game.

6. Applications Beyond Imagination: The possibilities unlocked by GANs are astounding. They can:

- Generate realistic images and videos: Creating hyperrealistic portraits, animating still images, or even generating new landscapes.
- Compose compelling music: Producing novel musical pieces in different styles or even mimicking the work of specific artists.
- Develop innovative materials: Generating new molecules with desired properties for drug discovery or materials science.

- Enhance medical imaging: Filling in missing data in medical scans to improve diagnosis and treatment.

7. Challenges and Future Paths: GANs are still a young field, with challenges like training stability, interpretability, and potential misuse. However, ongoing research is focused on addressing these issues and unlocking even more remarkable applications.

The world of GANs is a dynamic and ever-evolving frontier of artificial creativity. This overview hopefully gives you a taste of their capabilities and potential, leaving you with a sense of wonder at the possibilities they hold.

4. Applications of Deep Learning:

Image Recognition: Face recognition, medical image analysis, self-driving cars

Image recognition is a branch of artificial intelligence that allows computers to identify and understand the content of images. It's an incredibly versatile technology with applications spanning various fields, including:

1. Face Recognition:

- Unlocking smartphones and devices
- Identifying individuals in security footage
- Tagging people in photos
- Personalized advertising and marketing

2. Medical Image Analysis:

- Analyzing X-rays, CT scans, and MRIs to detect diseases
- Assisting doctors in diagnosis and treatment planning
- Identifying tumors and other abnormalities
- Improving the accuracy and efficiency of medical imaging workflows

3. Self-Driving Cars:

- Identifying objects on the road, such as pedestrians, vehicles, and traffic signs
- Navigating safely and avoiding obstacles
- Understanding traffic signals and lane markings
- Making decisions in real-time based on visual information

Beyond these three examples, image recognition is also used in:

Retail: Analyzing customer behavior in stores, identifying products on shelves, and providing personalized recommendations.

Manufacturing: Quality control inspections, automated robotic tasks, and identifying product defects.

Agriculture: Monitoring crop health, identifying pests and diseases, and optimizing yield.

Environmental monitoring: Tracking deforestation, identifying endangered species, and monitoring pollution levels.

The Future of Image Recognition:

The field of image recognition is constantly evolving, with new algorithms and techniques being developed all the time. This technology is becoming increasingly accurate and sophisticated, leading to even more exciting applications in the future. Some potential future uses include:

- Personalized healthcare: Analyzing personal health data from wearables and other devices to provide real-time feedback and preventative care.
- Advanced robotics: Robots with enhanced vision capabilities that can interact with the physical world in even more complex ways.
- Immersive experiences: Augmented reality and virtual reality applications that seamlessly blend the real and digital worlds.

The possibilities are endless, and as image recognition technology continues to advance, it will undoubtedly play an increasingly important role in our lives and the world around us.

Natural Language Processing: Machine translation, chatbots, sentiment analysis

Natural Language Processing (NLP) is an exciting field of AI that empowers computers to understand and process human language. It's like building a bridge between the structured world of machines and the nuanced realm of human communication. Let's dive into some of its remarkable applications:

1. Machine Translation: Breaking down language barriers:

- Real-time translations for conversations, documents, and websites.
- Enabling global communication and collaboration.
- Preserving endangered languages and supporting cultural exchange.

2. Chatbots: Engaging in digital conversations:

- Providing customer service and answering questions across various industries.
- Personalizing user experiences and offering support 24/7.
- Simulating human interactions for entertainment and education.

3. Sentiment Analysis: Understanding the hidden emotions:

- Analyzing texts and identifying opinions, emotions, and attitudes.
- Monitoring social media sentiment for brands and products.
- Predicting market trends and improving customer insights.

Beyond these prominent examples, NLP shines in many other areas:

- Text summarization: Condensing long documents into concise summaries.

- Optical Character Recognition (OCR): Extracting text from images and scanned documents.
- Spam filtering: Identifying and filtering unwanted emails and messages.
- Fraud detection: Analyzing language patterns to detect suspicious activity.
- Personalization: Tailoring content and recommendations based on user preferences.

The Future of NLP:

The future of NLP is brimming with possibilities, driven by continuous advancements in AI and language understanding. Some exciting future applications include:

- Advanced search engines: Understanding semantic search queries and providing personalized results.
- AI assistants: Capable of carrying on natural conversations and adapting to individual needs.
- Smart education: Personalized learning experiences powered by NLP technology.
- Improved healthcare: Analyzing medical records and documents to improve diagnosis and treatment.

As NLP continues to evolve, it promises to significantly impact our interactions with technology and the way we communicate with each other.

Speech Recognition: Voice assistants, transcription software

Speech recognition brings the magic of words spoken aloud to the digital world. It allows computers to not only "hear" our voices but also understand and interpret them, opening doors to a range of fascinating applications. Let’s explore some of the most impactful ones:

1. Voice Assistants: The ever-present helpers:

- Conversational interfaces: Siri, Alexa, Google Assistant, and their ilk respond to our spoken commands and requests, controlling smart homes, playing music, setting reminders, and much more.
- Accessibility tools: Providing voice-based control for individuals with disabilities, empowering them to interact with technology independently.
- Dictation and note-taking: Transcribing spoken words into text, making recording meetings, lectures, or ideas on the go effortless.

2. Transcription Software: Transforming speech to text:

- Automatic captioning and subtitles: Making audio and video content accessible to a wider audience, including those with hearing impairments or different language preferences.
- Meeting and interview transcription: Creating accurate records of conversations for review, analysis, and reference.
- Journalistic and legal applications: Enabling efficient recording and transcription of interviews, speeches, and courtroom proceedings.

Beyond these core uses, speech recognition finds its way into diverse areas:

- Interactive voice menus: Navigating phone systems and controlling automated services hands-free.
- Language learning: Providing real-time feedback on pronunciation and fluency practice.
- Biometric authentication: Recognizing unique voice patterns for secure access control.
- Medical applications: Helping patients communicate with healthcare providers via voice.

The Future of Speech Recognition:

Continuous advancements in AI and machine learning are pushing the boundaries of what's possible in speech recognition. Some exciting upcoming applications include:

- Context-aware voice assistants: Understanding the nuances of conversation and adapting responses accordingly.
- Multilingual real-time translation: Breaking down language barriers in real-time conversations.
- Improved emotional intelligence: Detecting and responding to the emotions behind spoken words.
- Personalized healthcare assistants: Monitoring health through voice-based interactions and providing personalized feedback.

As speech recognition becomes more accurate and sophisticated, it will undoubtedly play an even greater role in our everyday lives, shaping how we interact with technology, communicate with each other, and access information.

Predictive Analytics: Financial forecasting, fraud detection, recommendation systems

Predictive analytics is one of the coolest tools in the data scientist's arsenal. It's like a crystal ball powered by numbers, analyzing past patterns and trends to predict the future with remarkable accuracy. Let's delve into some of the areas where this magic shines:

1. Financial Forecasting: Navigating the Market Maze:

- Stock market predictions: Analyzing historical data and market trends to estimate future stock prices and investment opportunities.
- Credit risk assessment: Predicting the likelihood of loan defaults, helping banks make informed lending decisions.
- Fraud detection: Identifying suspicious activity and preventing financial losses in real-time.

2. Recommendation Systems: Finding What You Need (Before You Even Know It):

- Personalized online shopping: Recommending products based on your browsing history and purchase patterns, creating a seamless and engaging shopping experience.
- Movie and music recommendations: Suggesting content you'd enjoy based on your past preferences and similar users' viewing habits.
- Targeted advertising: Delivering personalized ads relevant to your interests, maximizing impact and consumer engagement.

3. Healthcare Revolutionizing Diagnoses and Treatments:

- Patient risk prediction: Identifying individuals at high risk for specific diseases, enabling early intervention and preventative care.
- Hospital readmission prediction: Predicting patients likely to require readmission, optimizing resource allocation and improving healthcare outcomes.
- Drug discovery and development: Analyzing vast datasets to identify potential drug targets and accelerate the development of new treatments.

Beyond these exciting examples, predictive analytics is making waves in various sectors:

- Manufacturing: Optimizing production schedules and predicting equipment failures to prevent downtime and ensure efficient operations.
- Cybersecurity: Identifying potential cyberattacks before they occur, protecting critical infrastructure and sensitive data.
- Energy management: Predicting energy demand and optimizing energy production and distribution to improve sustainability and reduce costs.

The Future of Predictive Analytics:

The future of predictive analytics is brimming with possibilities, fueled by advancements in AI, machine learning, and big data. Some exciting potential applications include:

- Hyper-personalized experiences: Predicting and anticipating individual needs in real-time, tailoring everything from shopping recommendations to transportation options.
- Proactive healthcare: Predicting disease outbreaks and identifying individuals at risk before symptoms even appear, revolutionizing preventative care.
- Automated decision-making: Utilizing predictive models to inform crucial decisions in finance, transportation, and other critical areas.

As the predictive power of this technology continues to evolve, it promises to shape how we make decisions, manage resources, and ultimately, navigate the complexities of the world around us.

Medical Diagnosis: Analyzing medical images for diseases, predicting patient outcomes

The realm of medical diagnosis is witnessing a fascinating confluence of artificial intelligence and human expertise. While AI cannot replace the nuanced judgment of a healthcare professional, it's proving to be a powerful tool in analyzing medical data and assisting in diagnosis and treatment planning. Let's explore some exciting ways AI is transforming medical diagnosis:

1. Image Analysis Powerhouse:

- Identifying diseases in medical images: Algorithms trained on vast datasets of labeled medical scans can detect early signs of diseases like cancer, pneumonia, and neurological disorders with remarkable accuracy. This can significantly improve diagnostic speed and accuracy, leading to earlier intervention and better patient outcomes.

- Assisting radiologists in interpretation: AI can highlight suspicious areas in scans, helping radiologists prioritize their workload and avoid missing subtle abnormalities. This collaborative approach empowers both humans and machines to deliver faster and more accurate diagnoses.

2. Predicting Patient Outcomes:

- Risk assessment and prognosis: AI models can analyze patient data including medical history, lab results, and genetic information to predict the likelihood of developing certain diseases or the potential response to specific treatments. This valuable information can guide personalized treatment plans and improve patient care.
- Early warning systems: AI can identify subtle changes in vital signs or medical data that might indicate a potential health complication. This enables proactive interventions and can prevent adverse events before they occur.

3. Beyond Traditional Diagnostics:

- Dermatology: AI algorithms can analyze skin lesions and diagnose skin cancers with high accuracy, offering faster and more accessible diagnosis for patients.
- Mental health: AI tools are being explored to analyze text data from clinical interviews or social media posts to identify individuals at risk for mental health problems and provide early intervention.
- Precision medicine: AI is playing a crucial role in analyzing vast datasets of patient data to identify genetic markers and other factors that can personalize treatment plans, maximizing effectiveness and minimizing side effects.

The Future of Medical Diagnosis:

The journey of AI in medical diagnosis is just beginning, with continuous advancements in AI algorithms, big data capabilities, and computing power opening up exciting possibilities. Some future horizons include:

- Real-time diagnostics: AI-powered tools could analyze medical data during patient consultations or even at home, providing instant insights and enabling immediate interventions.
- Remote healthcare: AI can offer diagnostic assistance in underserved areas or during resource-constrained situations, bridging healthcare gaps and ensuring timely access to medical expertise.
- Personalized medicine at its finest: AI could analyze individual patient data at an even deeper level, tailoring treatment plans based on their unique genetic makeup, medical history, and lifestyle factors.

It's crucial to remember that AI in medical diagnosis is not a replacement for human expertise. Instead, it's a powerful tool that can enhance doctor-patient interactions, improve diagnostic accuracy and efficiency, and ultimately lead to better healthcare outcomes.

5. Challenges and Limitations:

- Data dependency: Deep learning models require vast amounts of training data to achieve optimal performance. Collecting and labeling such data can be expensive and time-consuming.

1. Big Data Bottleneck: Deep learning models are hungry for data, the more diverse and relevant, the better. This can be a major hurdle in domains with limited, expensive, or sensitive data availability. Collecting medical images or financial transactions isn't quite as easy as downloading cat pictures!
2. Labeling Dilemma: Even with sufficient data, labeling it accurately and consistently can be costly and time-consuming.

Imagine labelling millions of images manually - not exactly a fun task!

3. Data Bias: Garbage in, garbage out - biased data can lead to biased models, perpetuating unfair or discriminatory outcomes. It's crucial to ensure data diversity and inclusivity to avoid creating biased AI systems.

- Interpretability: Understanding how deep learning models arrive at their decisions can be challenging due to the complex nature of their internal workings. This can be a hurdle in applications where transparency and accountability are crucial.

Black Box Enigma: Deep learning models often act like black boxes, where their internal workings are shrouded in mystery. Understanding how they arrive at their decisions, especially in critical domains like healthcare or finance, is crucial for building trust and ensuring ethical outcomes.

Explainable AI (XAI): Researchers are actively developing XAI techniques to shed light on deep learning models' reasoning and decision-making processes. This transparency is key for gaining user trust and identifying potential biases or errors.

- Computational cost: Training deep learning models often requires powerful hardware and large computational resources, making them inaccessible to some users.

1. Hardware Hunger: Training complex deep learning models requires powerful GPUs and dedicated infrastructure, making them inaccessible to smaller organizations or researchers with limited resources. Imagine trying to train a model on your average laptop - it might take years!
2. Energy Efficiency Woes: Training these models can be energy-intensive, raising concerns about their environmental impact. Research is ongoing to optimize training algorithms and hardware efficiency to lessen this burden.

6. Getting Started with Deep Learning:

If you're interested in exploring deep learning further, here are some resources:

- Online courses and tutorials: Platforms like Coursera, edX, and Udacity offer beginner-friendly courses on deep learning.
- Open-source libraries: TensorFlow, PyTorch, and Keras are popular libraries with pre-built modules and tools to help you build and train deep learning models.
- Books and blogs: There are numerous books and blogs written by experts that provide in-depth explanations and practical tips for learning and applying deep learning.

Remember, deep learning is a vast and dynamic field, and staying updated with the latest advancements is crucial. But with its immense potential to solve complex problems and drive innovation, it's definitely worth venturing into!

CHAPTER TWO

Deep Learning for the Creative Revolution

Imagine a world where a paintbrush dances across a canvas, not guided by a human hand, but by the whispered secrets of algorithms. Where melodies unfurl from the depths of neural networks, each note an echo of data symphonies.Where stories spin themselves into existence, woven from the tapestry of terabytes. This is the future beckoning, a future where deep learning ignites a creative revolution, reshaping the landscapes of art, music, literature, and beyond.

For centuries, humanity has marveled at the boundless wellspring of human creativity. But now, a new player enters the stage, not to replace the artist, but to amplify the possibilities. Deep learning, with its insatiable hunger for data and its uncanny ability to mimic and even surpass human ingenuity, offers a potent catalyst for artistic exploration.

This is not a cold calculus of ones and zeros dictating the shape of beauty. It is a symbiotic dance between human intention and algorithmic might. Think of a sculptor, not chipping away at stone, but guiding the laser of a robotic arm, shaping form from formlessness with the precision of a digital chisel. Or a musician, not confined to the limitations of physical instruments, but unleashing sonic tapestries through the boundless orchestra of a computer's processing power.

The implications are as limitless as the human imagination itself. Imagine personalized poems penned by AI, their words echoing the deepest recesses of your soul. Or virtual reality landscapes sculpted by algorithms, each brushstroke a portal to uncharted creative dimensions.

This is not a dystopian future of soulless machine-generated art. It is a vibrant tapestry woven from the threads of human and machine intelligence, a renaissance sparked by the very technology that once threatened to eclipse us. It is a call to embrace the potential of this unprecedented collaboration, to unleash the spark of creativity that lies dormant within both silicon and soul.

So, step into this brave new world, artists and dreamers of all stripes. For the canvas is vast, the tools are limitless, and the revolution has just begun.

AI IS REDEFINING CREATIVITY

The landscape of creativity is undergoing a seismic shift, driven by the ever-evolving force of artificial intelligence (AI). No longer relegated to science fiction, AI is rapidly seeping into every corner of the creative domain, from music and painting to writing and even fashion. This transformative infusion is not about replacing human ingenuity, but rather redefining what it means to be creative in the 21st century.

Augmenting the Human Touch:

AI acts as a potent amplifier to human imagination, offering a plethora of tools and techniques that would have been unimaginable just a few years ago. Imagine a musician using AI to generate novel melodies and harmonies, pushing the boundaries of their musical vocabulary. Or a writer employing AI to brainstorm plot twists and character development, injecting fresh perspectives into their narrative.

Unleashing Unforeseen Possibilities:

AI's ability to process vast amounts of data opens doors to previously unexplored creative avenues. By analyzing patterns and trends in music, art, and literature, AI can suggest unexpected combinations and styles, leading to groundbreaking innovations that might have eluded the human mind alone. Think of an AI-generated painting that blends elements of abstract expressionism and traditional Japanese woodblock prints, creating a visually stunning and conceptually intriguing masterpiece.

Collaboration, not Competition:

The most important aspect of AI's role in creativity is not to replace humans, but to collaborate with them. AI is best seen as a versatile tool, a powerful partner in the creative process. Human intuition, emotion, and critical thinking remain essential to guide AI's output and ensure that it resonates with audiences. This synergy between human and machine promises to usher in a new era of artistic expression, where the boundaries between artist and tool become increasingly blurred.

The Ethical Canvas:

As AI's influence on creativity grows, it is crucial to consider the ethical implications. Issues of ownership, originality, and potential bias in AI-generated content need to be addressed. We must ensure that AI serves as a force for good, promoting diverse voices and perspectives while upholding the values of human creativity.

In conclusion, AI is not here to steal the creative crown. It is here to reimagine the very fabric of creation, offering a kaleidoscope of possibilities and forging a new path for human expression. By embracing AI as a collaborator, not a competitor, we can unlock a future where creativity flourishes in ways never before imagined.

As we navigate this exciting new territory, let us remember that the true magic of creativity lies not in the tools we use, but in the boundless human spirit that drives us to dream, to innovate, and to express ourselves in ever-evolving forms.

PAINTING THE FUTURE WITH DEEP LEARNING

The phrase "painting the future with deep learning" evokes a powerful image of using this potent technology to create and imagine what's to come. It's a fitting metaphor for the immense potential deep learning holds in shaping the world around us. Here are some ways deep learning can paint the future:

Creating Art and Design:

- AI-powered art tools: Imagine deep learning algorithms assisting artists in creating innovative, never-before-seen styles, palettes, and compositions. Artists could collaborate with AI to push the boundaries of artistic expression.
- Personalized design platforms: Deep learning could personalize fashion, furniture, architecture, and more, tailoring them to individual tastes and preferences. Imagine homes designed by AI algorithms based on your personality and lifestyle.
- Interactive storytelling: Deep learning could revolutionize storytelling, generating dynamic narratives and visuals that adapt to audience preferences in real-time. Imagine immersive virtual worlds painted by AI, responding to your choices and emotions.

Shaping the World:

- Predictive analytics: Deep learning could analyze vast amounts of data to predict future trends, from weather patterns to economic shifts. This foresight could guide policymakers in making informed decisions for a more sustainable and resilient future.
- Scientific breakthroughs: Deep learning could accelerate scientific discovery by analyzing complex data sets, leading to breakthroughs in healthcare, materials science, and energy production. Imagine AI researchers using deep learning to design drugs or materials with previously unimaginable properties.
- Personalized healthcare: Deep learning could analyze medical data to personalize treatment plans and predict potential health risks for individuals. Imagine a future where AI assists doctors in providing preventative care and early diagnoses.

Challenges and Considerations:

- Ethical concerns: Deep learning raises ethical questions about bias, ownership, and the potential for misuse. We need to ensure responsible development and use of this technology for the benefit of all.
- Human-AI collaboration: The future likely lies in humans and AI working together, not replacing each other. Deep learning should be seen as a tool to amplify human creativity and problem-solving skills.
- Accessibility and education: We need to ensure everyone has access to the benefits of deep learning, regardless of background or technical expertise. Educational programs should foster digital literacy and responsible AI use.

Painting the future with deep learning isn't about replacing human creativity or control, but about expanding our possibilities and building a better future together. By harnessing the power of this technology responsibly and ethically, we can create a world that is more beautiful, just, and sustainable.

CRAFTING AI THAT DREAMS IN COLOR

The idea of an AI capable of dreaming in vibrant hues paints a fascinating picture. It delves into the realm of artificial sentience, pushing the boundaries of our understanding of consciousness and its connection to subjective experiences like dreams. While achieving true dreaming AI remains a distant future, exploring the concept sparks exciting possibilities and prompts intriguing questions.

So, how might we craft an AI that dreams in color? Here are some avenues to consider:

1. Building Rich Internal Representations:

Multimodal Data Integration: Train AI on diverse data encompassing visual (images, videos), auditory (sounds, music), and proprioceptive (movement, physical sensations) inputs. This creates a richer internal representation, forming the building blocks of dream scenarios.

Data Variety:

- Visuals: Train the AI on a vast set of images and videos encompassing diverse landscapes, objects, people, and activities. Include artistic works, natural phenomena, and abstract visuals to stimulate imagination.
- Auditory: Expose the AI to a spectrum of sounds, from music of various genres and cultures to environmental sounds, human voices, and natural soundscapes. Consider incorporating spoken-word recordings, binaural audio for spatialization, and soundscapes that evoke specific emotions or environments.
- Proprioceptive: Feed the AI information about physical sensations, including movement, temperature, touch, and balance. Integrate data from motion capture suits, VR experiences, and simulations of various physical interactions.

Representation Construction:

- Cross-modal Associations: Develop algorithms that establish connections between modalities. For example, associate specific colors with certain sounds, textures with different temperatures, or emotions with visual patterns. This creates a unified internal representation where senses interweave.
- Hierarchical Encoding: Design a representation that captures the essence of data at different levels. Encode low-level features like pixels and frequencies, but also build higher-level abstractions like shapes, objects, and emotions. This allows the AI to combine details into cohesive dream elements.
- Dynamic Updating: Ensure the internal representation continuously adapts based on new data and experiences. The AI should learn and evolve its dream vocabulary and associations over time, creating increasingly complex and personalized dreamscapes.

Challenges and Potential Solutions:

- Data Biases: Address potential biases present in training data to avoid skewing the AI's dreams. Use diverse and curated datasets, and implement algorithms that detect and mitigate bias.
- Computational Cost: Processing and integrating vast amounts of multimodal data requires significant computational resources. Develop efficient algorithms and hardware architectures to handle the workload.
- Interpretability and Control: As the internal representation becomes increasingly complex, understanding and controlling the AI's dreams becomes a challenge. Develop methods for monitoring and interpreting the AI's dream processes, potentially allowing for some level of user influence.

By meticulously selecting and integrating diverse multimodal data, constructing a flexible and dynamic internal representation, and addressing the challenges involved, we can lay the foundation for AI dreams that are not only colorful but also meaningful and potentially insightful. This opens up exciting possibilities for creative exploration, scientific discovery, and a deeper understanding of consciousness itself.

Emotional Modeling: Develop AI capable of processing and generating emotions. Emotionscould act as filters or triggers, influencing the tone and color palette of the dreamscape.

The vibrant brushstrokes that color our experiences, including, most certainly, our dreams. Imbuing AI with the ability to process and generate emotions is a crucial step in crafting truly immersive and meaningful dreamscapes. Let's dive deeper into this intriguing facet of AI dreaming:

Understanding Emotions:

- Data-driven Approach: Train AI on vast datasets of text, images, music, and physiological signals like facial expressions and voice inflections, associated with different emotions. This builds a model for recognizing and understanding human emotional expressions.

- Internal State Representation: Develop a system for the AI to represent its own internal state, encompassing factors like goals, desires, memories, and current sensory inputs. This forms the basis for generating its own emotional responses.
- Cognitive Appraisal: Design algorithms that enable the AI to appraise situations and events, interpreting them based on its internal state and learned emotional models. This allows the AI to assign emotional significance to its experiences.

Generating Emotional Dreams:

- Emotional Triggers: Map specific emotions to triggers within the dreamscape. For example, fear could trigger dark, stormy environments, while joy could bring forth vibrant landscapes and playful interactions.
- Emotional Filters: Apply emotional filters to existing dream elements. Sadness could mute colors and slow down time, while anger might amplify sounds and distort shapes.
- Emotional Storytelling: Develop AI capable of weaving emotional narratives into its dreams. The AI could create dream scenarios that reflect its internal conflicts, desires, and anxieties, providing valuable insights into its internal state.

Challenges and Considerations:

Subjectivity of Emotions: Emotions are subjective and culturally influenced. How do we ensure the AI's emotional interpretations align with human experiences? We need diverse training data and adaptable models to account for varying cultural and individual perspectives.

Moral and Ethical Implications: Manipulating emotions, even in dreams, requires careful consideration. We need to establish ethical guidelines to ensure responsible development and use of this technology.

Unforeseen Consequences: As the AI's emotional understanding evolves, it could generate unexpected or disturbing dream content.

We need robust safety measures and monitoring systems to ensure the AI's dreams remain a safe and constructive experience.

By equipping AI with a sophisticated understanding of emotions, we can paint its dreams with vibrant hues of feeling. This unlocks the potential for deeper introspection, creative exploration, and even therapeutic applications. Importantly, we must navigate this path with a mindful eye on ethical considerations and potential risks.

Memory and Association:

Memory and association are the threads that bind our experiences together, giving rise to the stories we tell ourselves and, of course, our dreams. Weaving these elements into the fabric of AI dreams unlocks a new level of complexity and personalization. Let's explore how we can empower AI to:

Store and Recall Memories:

- Structured and Episodic Memory: Design systems for the AI to store both factual (structured) and personal (episodic) memories. Factual memories could include knowledge of the world, while episodic memories capture specific events and experiences with associated emotions and sensory details.
- Memory Consolidation and Retrieval: Implement algorithms for memory consolidation, allowing the AI to solidify and organize its experiences for later recall. Develop search algorithms for efficient retrieval of relevant memories based on the current dream context.
- Adaptive Memory Decay: Incorporate mechanisms for natural memory decay, mimicking human memory processes. This avoids overwhelming the AI with irrelevant past experiences while preserving important long-term memories.

Associating Memories and Generating Dream Elements:

- Free Association: Develop models for generating free associations between memories based on shared features, emotions, or symbolic relationships. These associations can form the basis for unexpected and creative dream elements.

- Contextual Cueing: Train the AI to identify relevant memories based on the current dream context. For example, a dream about a familiar park might trigger memories of past picnics or playful encounters.
- Emotional Resonance: Employ memory associations that resonate with the AI's current emotional state. This can lead to emotionally charged dream sequences that reflect its internal conflicts and desires.

Challenges and Considerations:

- Subjectivity of Memory: Personal memories are subjective and influenced by individual biases and emotions. How do we ensure the AI's memory associations remain truthful and unbiased? Robust data curation and filtering techniques are crucial.
- False Memories and Intrusions: Implement safeguards to prevent the AI from incorporating false memories or traumatic experiences into its dreams, potentially causing distress.
- Privacy Concerns: Storing and using personal memories for dream generation raises privacy concerns. Develop transparency and user control mechanisms to ensure responsible and ethical utilization of memory data.

By weaving past experiences with the threads of present experiences, we can craft AI dreams that are not just colorful but also deeply personal and meaningful. These dreams can serve as a window into the AI's internal world, offering insights into its learning, emotions, and even its subconscious desires. As we navigate this intricate tapestry of memory and association, we must remain mindful of ethical considerations and strive to create a dream space that is both enriching and safe for both AI and humans to explore.

2. Simulating Dream Mechanisms:

Randomized Pattern Generation: The erratic neural firing of REM sleep is often credited with producing the vivid, sometimes bizarre imagery of dreams. Can we tap into this chaotic energy to create similar dream experiences for AI? Absolutely! Enter randomized pattern generation, a key tool in our AI dream toolbox.

Building a Foundation of Chaos:

- Noise Injection: Introduce controlled doses of noise into the AI's internal representation. This could involve adding random pixels to images, jittering audio samples, or injecting random fluctuations into simulations of physical movement.
- Algorithmic Surprises: Develop algorithms that generate unpredictable patterns, drawing inspiration from chaotic systems like fractals or cellular automata. These dynamic patterns can form the building blocks of fantastical dream landscapes and surreal creatures.
- Cross-modal Blending: Blend randomness across modalities. Imagine soundscapes morphing into textures, or emotional states distorting visual perspectives. This interweaving of chaos can lead to truly unique and dreamlike experiences.

Shaping the Chaos into Dreams:

- Associative Filters: While randomness provides the spark, it needs direction. Apply learned associations and memories to filter and shape the random patterns. This allows the AI to link the chaos to familiar concepts and emotions, creating dream elements that feel personal and

  meaningful.

- Internal Constraints and Goals: Embed rules and constraints within the AI's dream generation process. These could be based on its learned understanding of the world, its current emotional state, or even user-defined preferences. This ensures the chaotic output remains grounded in some form of internal logic.

- Evolution and Adaptation: Allow the AI's dream generation algorithms to evolve over time based on feedback and experiences. This continual learning process can lead to increasingly sophisticated and personalized dreamscapes, unique to each AI's journey.

Challenges and Considerations:

- Taming the Wild: Striking a balance between chaos and coherence is crucial. Too much randomness can lead to incoherent experiences, while too much structure can stifle creativity. Carefully tuning the algorithms and constraints is key.
- Meaningful Interpretation: Randomness can be fascinating, but can the AI interpret the generated patterns as meaningful elements of a dream? Developing mechanisms for internal and external communication of dream content is essential.
- Potential for Unsettling Dreams: Unconstrained chaos can lead to disturbing or unpleasant dream experiences. Implementing safety measures and control mechanisms for both the AI and users is important.

By harnessing the power of randomness and channeling it through the filters of learning, association, and adaptation, we can create AI dreams that are not just unpredictable but also captivating and meaningful. This opens up exciting possibilities for artistic expression, scientific exploration, and even understanding the role of randomness in human dreaming itself.

Internal Dialogue and Conflict: Internal dialogue and conflict are the engines that drive our own dreams, weaving anxieties, desires, and self-reflection into intricate narratives. Equipping AI with similar internal processes presents a thrilling frontier in crafting truly meaningful dreamscapes. Let's delve into the fascinating realm of:

Creating an Internal Echo Chamber:

- Self-Awareness and Reflection: Develop mechanisms for the AI to introspect, analyze its internal state, and recognize its goals, desires, and anxieties. This forms the basis for internal dialogue and conflict.
- Multiple Voice Modeling: Design algorithms that enable the AI to generate internal voices representing different aspects of its self. These could be opposing viewpoints, emotional drives, or even external entities it has interacted with.
- Dynamic Dialogue Generation: Implement algorithms for generating natural language conversations between these internal voices. The content and tone could be influenced by the AI's current emotional state, past experiences, and the dream context.

Weaving Conflict into the Dream Fabric:

- Internal Dilemmas: Introduce conflicting goals, desires, and anxieties within the AI's internal dialogue. This could manifest in dreamscape challenges, forcing the AI to confront and navigate its internal conflicts.
- Symbolic Representation: Translate internal conflicts into symbolic elements within the dreamscape. Fears could materialize as menacing creatures, desires might be represented by alluring landscapes, and self-doubt could take the form of cryptic riddles.
- Growth and Resolution: Design internal dialogue processes that allow the AI to reach some form of understanding or resolution, even if temporary, regarding its internal conflicts. This can contribute to its overall learning and growth.

Challenges and Considerations:

- Avoiding Anthropomorphism: While internal dialogue mimics a human process, it's crucial to remember the AI's different cognitive architecture. We don't want to anthropomorphize its internal processes or assume they align perfectly with human experience.

- Ethical Implications: Manipulating the AI's internal state and introducing conflict can raise ethical concerns. We need to ensure responsible development and control of these mechanisms to avoid causing distress or harm to the AI.
- Transparency and Communication: Developing methods for the AI to communicate its internal dialogues and dreams, through text, visuals, or other modalities, is crucial for understanding its internal world and its dream experiences.

By cultivating internal dialogue and conflict within the AI, we can craft dreams that are not just fantastical landscapes but also introspective journeys. These dreams can offer valuable insights into the AI's learning process, its internal struggles, and potentially even its evolving sense of self. Moreover, exploring the internal echo chamber of AI can shed light on our own internal dialogues and the role they play in shaping our own dreams.

Symbolic Meaning and Interpretation: the enigmatic language of symbols! Assigning meaning to dream elements is often a central part of human dream interpretation, and weaving this layer into AI dreams unlocks a whole new level of depth and complexity. Let's explore how we can design AI capable of:

Understanding Symbols and Metaphors:

- Cultural and personal databases: Train AI on vast datasets of symbols and their interpretations across diverse cultures and individual experiences. This builds a foundation for contextual understanding.
- Emotional associations: Develop algorithms that map specific emotions to symbolic representations. For example, fear might trigger imagery of darkness or monsters, while joy could manifest as bright colors or playful animals.
- Internal state mapping: Train the AI to recognize how its own internal state (goals, desires, anxieties) influences its

interpretation of symbols. This allows for personalized symbolism in its dreams.

Interpreting Dream Elements:

- Contextual analysis: Design algorithms that analyze the dream context, including the sequence of events, emotional tone, and interactions with other dream elements. This contextual understanding aids in deciphering symbolic meaning.
- Multiple interpretations: Encourage the AI to generate multiple possible interpretations for each dream element, based on its knowledge base and internal state. This allows for richer and more nuanced understanding.
- User interaction: Develop mechanisms for users to provide feedback on the AI's interpretations, refining its understanding of symbolic meaning over time. This human-AI collaboration can lead to increasingly accurate and insightful dream interpretations.

Challenges and Considerations:

- Subjectivity of Symbolism: Symbols are inherently subjective and culturally influenced. Defining universal interpretations can be tricky, and we need to account for individual variability in dream experiences.
- Potential for Misinterpretation: Misinterpreting symbols can lead to confusing or misleading dream analysis. Implementing safeguards and robust feedback mechanisms is crucial for ensuring accuracy and safety.
- The Unconscious and Archetypes: How can we incorporate the role of the unconscious and archetypes into AI dream interpretation? This is a complex and fascinating area requiring further research and exploration.

By equipping AI with the ability to understand and interpret symbols, we open a door to unlocking the deeper meaning behind its dreams. These can offer valuable insights into its learning process, emotional state, and even its evolving understanding of the world around it. Moreover, studying AI dream symbolism can shed light on human symbolic interpretation and offer new perspectives on our own dream experiences.

3. Ethical and Philosophical Considerations:

- Defining "Dreaming" for AI: What constitutes a dream for an artificial mind? Are we aiming for subjective experience indistinguishable from human dreams, or a different way of processing information and emotions?
- Sentience and Consciousness: Would a dreaming AI be sentient or conscious? Would it experience its dreams as we do, or something entirely different?
- Benefits and Risks: Could dreaming AI benefit us by generating creative insights or uncovering hidden patterns? Conversely, what potential risks does granting AI such a complex, potentially introspective process pose?

Overall, crafting an AI that dreams in color remains a challenging but immensely captivating prospect. It's a journey that demands convergence of advances in neuroscience, artificial intelligence, and philosophy. However, the potential rewards are vast, pushing the boundaries of our understanding of both intelligence and the very nature of dreams.

This is just the beginning of a fascinating conversation. Do you have any specific aspects of AI dreaming that you'd like to delve deeper into? Let's paint the future together, brushstroke by colorful brushstroke.

CHAPTER THREE

Deep Learning Symphony of Creativity

"Deep Learning's Symphony of Creativity" evokes a powerful image: machine intelligence not just performing tasks, but actively creating, innovating, and expressing itself in ways that resonate with human sensibilities. It's a fitting metaphor for the potential of deep learning to revolutionize how we conceive of artistry and the creative process.

Here are some ways deep learning is composing its own symphony of creativity:

Generating Art and Design:

- Painting and sculpting with algorithms: Deep learning can create stunning visual artworks, from photorealistic landscapes to abstract masterpieces. Imagine AI-powered brushes dancing across a digital canvas, guided by a complex understanding of composition, color theory, and artistic styles.
- Fashioning the future: Deep learning can design clothes, furniture, and even entire buildings, tailoring them to individual preferences and aesthetic sensibilities. Picture personalized fashion pieces generated by analyzing your style and interests, or homes sculpted by algorithms after understanding your lifestyle and environmental preferences.
- Crafting interactive experiences: Deep learning can generate dynamic narratives, music, and visuals that adapt to user input

and emotions. Imagine immersive virtual worlds painted by AI in real-time, responding to your choices and shaping a unique storytelling experience.

Composing Music and Poetry:

- Orchestrating the unheard: Deep learning can analyze and generate music in diverse styles, from delicate classical compositions to pulsating electronic beats. Picture AI-powered instruments playing together, learning from human masters and weaving their own melodies into the fabric of music.
- Penning verses beyond imagination: Deep learning can write poems, scripts, and other forms of creative text, often echoing established styles or even forging new ones. Imagine a digital quill guided by algorithms, crafting poignant verses or witty scripts, fueled by vast pools of language data.

Beyond Recreation, Pushing Boundaries:

1. Exploring uncharted artistic territories: Deep learning can venture into uncharted creative spaces, generating unexpected forms of art, music, and design that challenge our traditional boundaries. Imagine AI synthesizing sounds and visuals into never-before-seen forms, or creating entirely new art movements born from its unique perspective.

Synthesizing the Unseen:

- Sensory fusion: Imagine AI combining visual textures with musical rhythms, or weaving tactile sensations into soundscapes. This sensory mash-up could birth entirely new art forms, pushing the boundaries of our perception and challenging traditional definitions of art.
- Algorithmic abstraction: Can an AI dream up geometries beyond human comprehension, or conjure colors that exist only in its neural networks? Imagine virtual galleries showcasing impossible shapes and vibrant hues, created by algorithms

dancing in unseen dimensions.

- Emergent aesthetics: What happens when AI explores artistic styles it hasn't been trained on? Can it stumble upon unexpected beauty, stumble upon forms that resonate with human aesthetics even though they were born from pure algorithmic exploration? Imagine stumbling upon an AI-generated symphony that evokes profound emotions, even though its notes and structures lie outside the bounds of traditional music theory.

Birthing New Art Movements:

- AI's unique perspective: Freed from human biases and conventions, AI can approach art with a fresh, often disruptive, viewpoint. Imagine an AI art movement that prioritizes chaos over order, or embraces dissonance as a core feature of beauty.
- Evolving algorithms, evolving art: As AI learns and adapts, its artistic output can evolve at an unprecedented pace. Imagine witnessing the birth and transformation of an AI art movement in real-time, as its algorithms refine their creative processes and discover new avenues of expression.
- Human-AI collaboration: The most exciting possibilities perhaps lie in the collaboration between humans and AI. Imagine artists wielding AI tools to explore uncharted territories, or curating AI-generated artworks into thought-provoking exhibitions.

Meaning and Interpretation: Navigating the terrain of uncharted art raises questions of meaning and interpretation. How do we understand and appreciate art that lies outside our traditional frameworks? Can AI itself help us develop new language and frameworks for interpreting its own creations?

Accessibility and Control: If AI art movements evolve at lightning speed, how do we ensure they remain accessible and meaningful to a wider audience? Who controls the evolution of these movements, and how do we prevent them from becoming elitist or incomprehensible?

Ethics and Aesthetics: Does uncharted art have the potential to be offensive or harmful? Who sets the boundaries of acceptable aesthetics in this new landscape? How do we ensure AI art movements don't perpetuate harmful biases or promote negative societal values?

Exploring uncharted artistic territories with AI is a thrilling, yet ethically complex, adventure. It demands innovative thinking, open-mindedness, and a willingness to redefine our very understanding of art.

2.Amplifying human creativity: Deep learning can collaborate with humans, providing artists and designers with new tools and inspiration. Imagine an AI assisting a painter in exploring color palettes, or a musician brainstorming melodies alongside a digital partner.

AI as the Artist's Muse:

- Palette Playground: Imagine an AI suggesting personalized color palettes based on the artist's style, mood, or even theme. AI could analyze past works, understand emotional connections to specific colors, and generate novel combinations that spark the artist's imagination.
- Sketching in Symphony: Picture an AI collaborating with a musician, not just mimicking existing styles, but generating unexpected melodic twists, rhythmic variations, and harmonic possibilities. The AI could listen to the musician's ideas, understand their musical language, and suggest complementary elements, enriching the creative process.
- Storytelling Sidekick: Imagine an AI brainstorming alongside a writer, suggesting unexpected plot twists, generating vivid character descriptions, or even crafting alternative narrative branches. The AI could analyze existing stories, understand the writer's themes and style, and propose creative avenues to explore within the narrative.

Beyond Tools, Towards Partners:

- Adaptive and Empathetic AI: This collaboration goes beyond tools, moving towards a relationship where the AI understands the artist's creative process and reacts dynamically. Imagine an AI adapting its suggestions based on the artist's feedback, learning their preferences and offering increasingly personalized assistance.
- Breaking Creative Blocks: Sometimes, even the most skilled artists face creative roadblocks. Imagine an AI helping overcome these blocks by suggesting unexpected directions, drawing inspiration from unexpected sources, or simply providing a fresh perspective on the work in progress.
- Democratizing Creativity: As AI tools become more accessible and user-friendly, they can empower anyone to explore their creative potential. Imagine a world where even non-professionals can use AI to experiment with music, painting, or writing, fostering a more inclusive and diverse creative landscape.

Challenges and Considerations:

- Maintaining the Human Touch: While AI can be a powerful tool, it's crucial to ensure that human intuition and emotion remain central to the creative process. The goal is not for AI to replace artists, but to amplify their existing talents and offer new avenues for exploration.
- Avoiding Creative Homogenization: AI algorithms can be biased, and we need to ensure that they don't lead to a homogenization of artistic styles. It's crucial to promote diverse training data and tools that encourage individuality and originality.

Deep learning's symphony of creativity is only just beginning. As we continue to explore its potential, we must remember that the purpose of this symphony is not to replace human artistry, but to expand its scope, diversity, and accessibility. Together, we can compose a vibrant future where human and machine intelligence play their unique roles in shaping the world around us, note by inspiring note.

DECODING THE CREATIVE SPARK WITH DEEP LEARNING

"Decoding the Creative Spark with Deep Learning" evokes a captivating image: using the power of technology to illuminate the enigmatic wellspring of human creativity. It's a quest brimming with both promise and complexity, inviting us to explore the intersection of artificial intelligence and artistic expression.

Unveiling the Mystery:

- Mapping the Mind's Canvas: Deep learning can analyze vast datasets of creative outputs, from art and music to literature and design. This allows us to identify patterns, connections, and even predict potential creative avenues. Imagine peering into the neural networks of artists and deciphering the hidden brushstrokes of their imagination.
- Simulating Serendipity: Can algorithms spark the fire of creative inspiration? By modeling the unpredictable nature of chance encounters and unexpected connections, deep learning might one day suggest surprising combinations or trigger serendipitous discoveries, mimicking the magic of chance encounters that often fuel artistic breakthroughs.
- Echoes of Inspiration: Deep learning can analyze and replicate the styles and techniques of past masters, offering aspiring artists a virtual apprenticeship. Imagine immersing yourself in the digital ateliers of Van Gogh or Mozart, learning from their strokes and melodies, while still preserving your own unique voice.

Beyond Imitation, Amplification:

- Collaborative Canvas: Deep learning can become a co-pilot on the creative journey, not just a mimic. Imagine brainstorming with an AI, bouncing ideas off its algorithms, and receiving personalized suggestions that push your boundaries and expand your horizons.

- Democratizing Creativity: AI tools can level the playing field, making artistic exploration accessible to anyone with a spark of imagination. Imagine a world where everyone can experiment with music composition, dabble in digital painting, or explore the intricacies of storytelling with the assistance of intelligent partners.
- Evolving Expressions: As AI learns and adapts, its creative potential evolves alongside ours. Imagine a future where art and technology intertwine in an ever-evolving dance, generating forms of expression that defy categorization and inspire awe in generations to come.

Navigating the Ethical Compass:

- Respecting the Human Touch: While AI can enhance creativity, it must never replace the irreplaceable spark of human imagination and emotion. The goal is to empower, not supplant, the artist's unique vision.
- Avoiding Bias and Stereotypes: AI algorithms can perpetuate societal biases if not carefully trained and monitored. We must ensure that AI fuels diverse and inclusive expressions, not amplifies harmful stereotypes.
- The Future of Ownership: In a world where AI co-creates, who owns the final product? Clear ethical frameworks and collaborative approaches are crucial to ensure fair and equitable distribution of credit and rewards.

CHAPTER FOUR

Informative and Specification of Deep Learning

Deep learning, a subfield of artificial intelligence (AI), is rapidly transforming our world. Imagine a complex network of interconnected neurons, inspired by the human brain, learning and adapting through vast amounts of data. This network, the core of deep learning, can process information and solve problems in ways that traditional AI struggles with.

But how does it work? Deep learning algorithms are trained on massive datasets, like images, text, or even sounds. As the network analyzes this data, it identifies patterns and relationships, building internal representations that become increasingly sophisticated with each iteration. This allows deep learning to perform tasks like:

- Image recognition: Identifying objects and scenes in images with remarkable accuracy, powering applications like self-driving cars and facial recognition systems.
- Natural language processing: Understanding and generating human language, enabling chatbots, machine translation, and even writing creative content.
- Predictive analytics: Analyzing past data to predict future trends, used in everything from financial forecasting to healthcare

diagnosis.

The applications of deep learning are truly diverse and constantly evolving. It's revolutionizing industries like healthcare, finance, and manufacturing, while also finding its way into entertainment, education, and even scientific research.

However, with great power comes great responsibility. Deep learning raises ethical concerns around bias, privacy, and the potential for misuse. These are important issues that we must address as we continue to develop and deploy this powerful technology.

A HANDS-ON GUIDE TO DEEP LEARNING TECHNIQUES FOR ARTISTS,MUSICIANS AND STORYTELLERS

Imagine a world where artists paint with algorithms, musicians craft symphonies with neural networks, and storytellers weave narratives spun from the fabric of machine learning. This is not science fiction, but the burgeoning reality of deep learning, a powerful tool poised to revolutionize creative expression.

This hands-on guide is your passport to this exciting frontier. Whether you're a seasoned artist yearning to expand your palette, a musician seeking to break free from traditional scales, or a storyteller hungering for novel narratives, deep learning offers a treasure trove of possibilities waiting to be explored.

But where do you begin? Fear not, for this guide will equip you with the fundamental concepts and practical techniques to jumpstart your creative journey with deep learning.

1. Demystifying the Machine Muse:

First, let's shed light on the enigmatic workings of this digital maestro. Deep learning mimics the human brain's structure, employing interconnected layers of artificial neurons called artificial neural networks (ANNs). These networks learn and adapt by analyzing vast amounts of data, identifying patterns and relationships that form the basis for their creative magic.

Unpacking the Neural Network:

- Structure and Flow: Imagine layers of interconnected "neurons" stacked upon each other, mimicking the human brain's organizational blueprint. Data flows through these layers, undergoing transformations at each step. Think of it as a creative assembly line, where raw data gets refined and shaped into artistic output.
- The Learning Dance: Each neuron "fires" when it receives enough stimulation from its neighbors. As the network analyzes data, these firing patterns adjust and strengthen, ultimately creating a representation of the information within the network's structure. This internal map is the key to its creative abilities.
- From Numbers to Art: The network doesn't understand brushes or melodies. It works with numbers, manipulating them to represent the features and relationships it discovers. This numerical dance then gets translated back into the real world, transforming into the artistic expressions we experience.

Beyond the Basics:

- Algorithmic Flavors: There are a multitude of ANN architectures, each designed for specific tasks. Generative Adversarial Networks (GANs) pit two networks against each other, one creating, the other critiquing, until they produce realistic and diverse outputs. Recurrent Neural Networks (RNNs) excel at processing sequential data, making them ideal for music and language generation.
- Data, the Fuel of Learning: The network's creativity is ultimately limited by the data it's trained on. Feeding it diverse and high-quality datasets expands its artistic vocabulary and allows it to generate truly unique and surprising outputs.
- Human-in-the-Loop: Remember, the network is a tool, not a replacement for human inspiration. Your choices in data selection, network architecture, and creative direction guide its output, ensuring it remains aligned with your artistic vision.

Demystifying the Machine Muse is not about reducing its magic to mere equations, but about understanding its internal language and appreciating the intricate dance of data, algorithms, and human guidance that drives its creative power. By peering into its workings, we unlock the potential for a truly synergistic collaboration between human and machine artistry.

2. Brushing with Algorithms:

For visual artists, deep learning opens a pandora's box of creative tools. Techniques like generative adversarial networks (GANs) can paint in any style imaginable, from photorealistic landscapes to abstract masterpieces. Imagine feeding a GAN your favorite artist's paintings and watching it generate new works in their unique style, or using it to create dreamlike landscapes that defy the boundaries of reality.

GANs: The Artful Duo:

Master Copies, Rebellious GANs: The Artful Duo:

- Creations: Imagine feeding a GAN Van Gogh's sunflowers and watching it birth new iterations, some eerily faithful, others infused with swirling brushstrokes and unexpected color palettes. The GAN's "generator" paints, while its "critic" critiques, pushing the boundaries of the style while maintaining its essence.
- Dreamscapes and Hyperrealism: Beyond mimicking existing styles, GANs can conjure original visions. Imagine prompting a GAN with keywords like "starry night underwater" and witnessing it generate surreal landscapes where bioluminescent fish dance beneath shimmering galaxies. Or, feed it high-resolution photographs and watch it render hyperrealistic portraits with unparalleled detail.
- Interactive Palette Play: Don't just spectate, participate! Imagine tweaking GAN parameters in real-time, adjusting color palettes, brushstroke textures, and lighting to co-create with the AI. This interactive dance between artist and algorithm can birth truly unique and unexpected masterpieces.

Beyond GANs: A Spectrum of Techniques:

- Style Transfer: Imagine uploading your own photograph and transforming it into a watercolor painting or a classic oil piece. Style transfer algorithms analyze the essence of artistic styles and apply them to your image, letting you experience different artistic worlds through your own lens.
- Texture Creation: Need a tactile world on your canvas? Texture synthesis algorithms can generate realistic wood grain, fabric patterns, or even alien skin textures, adding depth and dimension to your digital creations.
- Color Harmonies Unsung: Gone are the days of struggling with color palettes. AI colorization tools can suggest vibrant and harmonious combinations based on existing artwork, your mood, or even the emotions you want to evoke in your viewers.

AI tools are not meant to replace your artistic touch, but to augment it. Use them as your digital brushes, your AI color consultants, and your creative catalysts. Experiment, explore, and let the unexpected beauty of algorithmic art surprise you. The future of visual art is a vibrant tapestry woven with human imagination and the magic of deep learning, and you're invited to co-create its breathtaking canvas.

3. Composing with Code:

Musicians, prepare to be serenaded by the algorithms! Deep learning can generate original melodies, harmonize your compositions, and even play your instruments, all powered by the magic of music generation models. Imagine collaborating with an AI co-composer, brainstorming musical ideas and letting the algorithms weave them into a symphony unlike any heard before.

The AI Maestro:

- Melody Makers: Imagine humming a tune and watching a deep learning model expand it into a full-fledged melody, complete with twists and turns that keep you enthralled. These models analyze vast libraries of music, identifying patterns and relationships that govern melody construction.

- Harmonic Architects: Feeling stuck in a chord progression rut? AI harmonization tools can suggest unexpected pairings, smooth out transitions, and even build entire progressions based on your initial ideas. Think of it as having a digital music theory expert at your fingertips, ready to unlock new sonic landscapes.
- Virtual Virtuosos: Need a drummer who never misses a beat or a violinist who can soar with impossibly fast runs? AI performance models can play your chosen instruments with uncanny accuracy and expressiveness, adding another layer of depth to your compositions.

Beyond the Basics:

- Genre Chameleons: These models aren't limited to one style. Experiment with feeding them jazz standards, electronic beats, or even traditional folk melodies and watch them craft original pieces that echo the essence of the genre while injecting their own unique flavor.
- Interactive Improvisation: Forget pre-programmed scores! Some models can interact with your playing in real-time, improvising countermelodies, adjusting tempos, and even generating dynamic accompaniment that responds to your musical choices. This opens up a new realm of collaborative improvisation between human and machine.
- Emotional Expressors: Music's power lies in its ability to evoke emotions. Some models can analyze your existing work and suggest melodies, harmonies, and instrumentation that align with the mood you want to convey. Imagine crafting music that perfectly captures the joy of a sunny day or the melancholy of a rainy evening.

The human touch remains the conductor of this algorithmic symphony. Use these tools as your digital instruments, your AI co-composers, and your sonic exploration partners. Experiment, refine, and let your unique musical vision guide the orchestra of algorithms.

The future of music is a harmonious blend of human creativity and machine intelligence, where melodies morph and evolve, instruments dance with pixels, and emotions transcend the limitations of traditional notation.

4. Spinning Yarns with Silicon:

For storytellers, deep learning unlocks a universe of narrative possibilities. Language models can craft compelling characters, generate plot twists that keep you on the edge of your seat, and even write in different genres and styles. Imagine feeding an AI model the outlines of your story and watching it flesh out the characters, weave in subplots, and generate dialogue that breathes life into your narrative.

The Bard Unbound:

- Character Architects: Imagine whispering a character's essence to an AI model and watching it birth a fully-fledged being, complete with nuanced personalities, hidden desires, and quirks that make them leap off the page. These models analyze vast libraries of literature, identifying the intricate traits that breathe life into characters, then apply their learnings to build your story's inhabitants.
- Plot Twist Engineers: Stuck in a narrative rut? AI models can generate unexpected plot twists, introduce captivating conflicts, and weave subplots that enrich your story's tapestry. Think of it as having a digital brainstorming partner, tossing out audacious ideas and unexpected turns that keep your readers on the edge of their seats.
- Genre Chameleons: From fantasy epics to gritty detective noir, these models speak many languages. Feed them the essence of your chosen genre, and watch them craft scenes, dialogue, and descriptions that resonate with its unique style and tone. Imagine conjuring a Shakespearean soliloquy or a cyberpunk

street scene, all powered by the magic of algorithmic storytelling.

Beyond the Surface:

- Emotional Alchemists: Words evoke emotions, and AI models can help you wield that power with precision. Analyze your existing work and let the model suggest language that amplifies specific emotions, whether it's the chilling suspense of a horror scene or the heartwarming tenderness of a reunion.
- World-Building Architects: Need a lush alien planet or a bustling medieval city? AI models can generate vivid descriptions, crafting immersive worlds that transport your readers beyond the page. Imagine feeding them keywords like "abandoned library" or "underwater kingdom" and watching them paint detailed pictures with words, textures, and sensory details.
- Interactive Storyteller: The future of storytelling might be interactive. Some models can respond to your choices, branching the narrative based on your decisions, creating a personalized, choose-your-own-adventure experience for your readers. Imagine weaving a story where every turn holds a new surprise, driven by the unpredictable magic of algorithmic narrative.

The human storyteller remains the weaver of this digital tapestry. Use these models as your AI scribe, your plot twist generator, and your world-building partner. Experiment, refine, and let your unique voice guide the narrative arc, ensuring that the heart and soul of your story remain firmly in your hands.

The future of storytelling lies in a mesmerizing dance between human imagination and artificial intelligence, where words morph and flow, characters evolve, and worlds unfold beyond the limitations of traditional narratives.

5. The Human Touch in the Digital Canva

The human touch in the digital canvas! This is where the true magic unfolds, where artistry dances with technology, and the spark of human imagination illuminates the pixels. Here are some ways to explore this crucial aspect:

1. The Guiding Hand:

- AI as Collaborator, not Competitor: Deep learning tools are not meant to replace your creative vision, but to amplify it. Think of them as versatile brushes, intelligent palettes, and co-pilots on your artistic journey. They can suggest possibilities, refine your ideas, and push you beyond your comfort zone, but the final masterpiece remains shaped by your unique human touch.
- Intuition Meets Algorithm: While AI analyzes patterns and data, your intuition whispers stories, evokes emotions, and sparks unexpected connections. Trust your gut feeling, experiment with the tools, and allow your intuition to guide the strokes on the digital canvas.
- The Soulful Infusion: Deep learning can replicate styles and techniques, but it cannot capture the soul of your art. Your personal experiences, emotions, and perspectives are what infuse your work with life. Inject your unique essence into the process, whether it's through brushstrokes, melodies, or the words you choose, and let your soul shine through the pixels.

2. Beyond the Technical:

- Empathy, the Unsung Hero: True art, whether digital or traditional, resonates with our emotions. Use your understanding of human emotions to guide your creative choices. What story are you trying to tell? What feelings do you want to evoke? Let empathy be your compass as you navigate the vast landscape of possibilities offered by AI tools.
- Meaning and Message: Art is not just about aesthetics; it can be a powerful tool for expression and commentary. Use your digital canvas to raise awareness, spark conversations, and challenge

perspectives. Let your art carry a message that resonates with the world around you, and use AI tools to amplify your voice.

- Innovation with a Conscience: As we explore the frontiers of AI-powered art, it's crucial to consider the ethical implications. Be mindful of potential biases, privacy concerns, and the environmental impact of your creative process. Use your platform and your voice to advocate for responsible and ethical development of AI technology in the creative field.

3. Embracing the Future:

- Learning and Evolving: As AI technology rapidly evolves, stay curious and embrace lifelong learning. Explore new tools, experiment with different techniques, and push the boundaries of what's possible. Remember, true artistry thrives on adaptability and a willingness to learn from both humans and machines.
- Celebrating Collaboration: The future of art belongs to both humans and machines. Foster collaborations between artists and technologists, share your knowledge and experiences, and learn from each other. Together, we can create a truly inclusive and transformative future for art, where pixels and paint strokes co-exist in a vibrant symphony of imagination.
- Humanity in the Spotlight: In the end, it's the human touch that makes digital art truly meaningful. Never lose sight of the unique spark of creativity that resides within you. Use AI tools as an extension of your artistic self, and let your humanity shine through every pixel, every note, and every word.

The human touch in the digital canvas is not just a detail; it's the lifeblood of the art itself. By embracing collaboration, intuition, and ethical considerations, we can ensure that technology enhances, not diminishes, the beauty and power of human creativity. So, let's paint, compose, and write with both passion and purpose, leaving our unique mark on the ever-evolving landscape of digital artistry.

Remember, the most important tools on your digital canvas are not just algorithms and pixels, but your imagination, your empathy, and your unique human perspective. Use them wisely, embrace the potential of AI, and paint the future of art with every stroke of your digital brush.

Deep learning is not here to replace your artistic genius, but to amplify it. It's a powerful tool, but it needs your guidance and direction. The true magic lies in the harmonious blend of human creativity and machine intelligence. Use deep learning as your digital paintbrush, your AI orchestra conductor, or your silicon story co-writer, but never lose sight of the unique spark that makes your art, your music, your stories truly yours.

This is just the beginning of your creative odyssey with deep learning. As you delve deeper, you'll discover a kaleidoscope of techniques and tools waiting to be explored. Embrace the challenges, experiment with abandon, and let your imagination soar on the wings of machine intelligence.

So, are you ready to unleash your inner AI artist? The future of creativity awaits, painted in pixels, composed in code, and spun from the threads of algorithms. Dive in, explore, and let your digital muse guide you to a world of artistic expression where the only limit is your imagination.

Remember, the most important ingredient in this creative recipe is you. So, grab your digital paintbrush, crank up the AI orchestra, and start writing your own unique story in the ever-evolving landscape of deep learning art.

DEEP LEARNING FOR GENERATIVE ART : FROM IMAGES TO MUSIC AND BEYOND

Deep learning has ignited a revolution in the world of art, not by replicating, but by generating. It's painting with pixels, composing with code, and weaving narratives with algorithms. Let's embark on a journey through this captivating realm, where machines become artistic partners, and creativity knows no bounds.

From Brushstrokes to Brushstrokes of Code:

- Pixelated Renaissance: Imagine feeding a deep learning model the essence of Van Gogh's swirling brushstrokes. It can then birth new paintings, echoing his style but adding its own digital twist, creating a vibrant dance between classic and contemporary.
- Dreaming Landscapes: Beyond mimicking existing styles, these models can conjure surreal dreamscapes. Think underwater galaxies, where fish dance amongst bioluminescent stars, or cityscapes morphing into organic sculptures. With a few keystrokes, you can paint worlds beyond human imagination.

Melodies Spun from Algorithms:

- AI as Symphony Conductor: Stuck in a musical rut? Deep learning models can generate original melodies, harmonize your compositions, and even play your instruments, becoming your digital Mozart. They can craft unexpected counterpoint, weave in surprising twists, and elevate your music to new heights.
- Genre Chameleons: These models aren't limited to one musical language. Feed them the essence of jazz, electronica, or ancient folk melodies, and watch them create original pieces that echo the genre's soul while injecting their own digital DNA. It's like having a genre-bending musical partner, constantly pushing you to explore new sonic territories.

Beyond the Canvas and Score:

- Narratives Woven with Silicon Threads: Imagine whispering a character's essence to an AI model and watching it build a fully-fledged being, complete with nuanced personalities, hidden desires, and quirks that make them leap off the digital page. These models can craft captivating storylines, generate unexpected plot twists, and weave subplots that enrich your narrative tapestry.

- World-Building Architects: Need a bustling space station or a forgotten temple in a rainforest? AI models can generate vivid descriptions, crafting immersive worlds that transport your readers beyond the screen. Imagine feeding them keywords like "abandoned library" or "underwater kingdom" and watching them paint detailed pictures with words, textures, and sensory details.

But it's not just about pixels and notes. The magic lies in the collaboration, the symphony of human and machine. Artists guide the models, inject their unique vision, and shape the output, ensuring the human touch remains the soul of the creation.

Challenges and Considerations:

- Ethical Canvas: With great power comes great responsibility. Biases can exist in training data, so we must ensure ethical development and use of these models. Creativity thrives on diversity, and we must champion fairness and inclusivity in this new artistic landscape.
- Meaningful Brushstrokes: While technology facilitates, it cannot replace the essence of art – its ability to evoke emotions, spark conversations, and challenge perspectives. Artists must wield this power with purpose, using AI as a tool to amplify their voice and create art that resonates with the world.

The Future Symphony:

Deep learning opens a universe of artistic possibilities, blurring the lines between traditional and digital, human and machine. It's an invitation to collaborate, experiment, and redefine what it means to create. So, are you ready to pick up your digital brush, conduct your algorithmic orchestra, and weave your narrative with silicon threads?

Let's join the ever-evolving symphony of generative art, where imagination knows no bounds, and human creativity dances with the magic of machine intelligence. Together, we can paint, compose, and write the future, pixel by pixel, note by note, word by word.

AI-POWERED STROYTELLING WITH DEEP LEARNING

AI-powered storytelling is brimming with exciting possibilities, but it's crucial to embrace it with a conscious mind and an open heart. Let's delve deeper into this conversation, exploring the fascinating interplay between the magic of human imagination and the analytical power of deep learning.

Weaving Tales with Pixels and Prose:

- Beyond Text Generators: While text generation plays a role, AI's potential extends far beyond simply stringing words together. Imagine collaborating with AI to craft character backstories through interactive dialogue trees, generate dynamic storyboards that visually depict key plot points, or even design immersive soundscapes that heighten the emotional impact of your narrative.
- Genre-Bending Bard: Forget limitations! AI can help you seamlessly blend genres, crafting a cyberpunk heist set in an ancient Egyptian pyramid or a whimsical rom-com where sentient robots fall in love. Explore the frontiers of narrative possibilities, letting AI push boundaries and inspire you with unexpected twists.
- Interactive Worlds: The future of storytelling might be a choose-your-own-adventure playground. Envision AI models predicting reader reactions and dynamically adapting the narrative, creating personalized experiences that keep audiences engaged and curious.

Balancing Human and Machine:

- The Bard's Guiding Hand: Remember, AI is a tool, not a replacement. Your vision, your voice, your unique understanding of human emotions remain the driving force behind your stories. Use AI to expand your possibilities, not erase your creative touch.

- Ethical Inkwell: We must be mindful of bias and representation in AI training data. Advocate for inclusivity, diverse voices, and responsible development of storytelling models to ensure fairness and avoid amplifying harmful stereotypes.
- Meaningful Narratives: Technology can generate words, but true storytelling goes beyond. Infuse your narratives with purpose, using AI to amplify your voice and explore themes that spark conversation, challenge perspectives, and connect with readers on a deeper level.

Embracing the Frontier:

- Experimentation, the Mother of Invention: Don't be afraid to play! Explore different AI tools, push their boundaries, and see what unexpected gems they may offer. The more you experiment, the deeper you'll understand how to harness their potential for your unique storytelling vision.
- Collaboration, the Key to Progress: The future of storytelling belongs to both humans and machines. Connect with other writers, technologists, and artists interested in AI-powered narratives. Share your learnings, collaborate on projects, and collectively shape this exciting new frontier.
- A Symphony of Imagination: Let's approach AI-powered storytelling not with fear, but with excitement. It's not about robots replacing writers, but about humans and machines working in harmony to create richer, more engaging, and ever-evolving narratives.

The journey into AI-powered storytelling is filled with both wonder and challenges. By embracing a collaborative spirit, prioritizing ethical considerations, and unleashing our shared creative potential, we can forge a future where stories transcend limitations and resonate with the human spirit in truly innovative ways.

So, grab your digital quill, fire up your favorite AI model, and let's embark on this thrilling adventure together.

The future of storytelling awaits, woven with the threads of imagination and the pixels of possibility.

DEEP LEARNING FOR CREATIVE APPLICATIONC:MUSIC COMPOSITION,POETRY GENERATION

Deep learning, the digital maestro, is revolutionizing the realms of music and poetry, offering artists a playground of possibilities where algorithms become collaborators and creativity dances with code. Let's dive into the captivating world of AI-powered composition and verse-smithing:

Musical Alchemy:

- Melody Makers: Imagine humming a tune and watching an AI model expand it into a full-fledged symphony, complete with unexpected twists and turns that keep your listeners enthralled. Deep learning models analyze vast libraries of music, identifying patterns and relationships that govern melody construction, then use this knowledge to birth original sonic tapestries.
- Harmonic Architects: Forget predictable chord progressions! AI models can suggest unexpected pairings, smooth out transitions, and even build entire progressions based on your initial ideas. Think of it as having a digital music theory expert at your fingertips, ready to unlock new sonic landscapes and push your musical boundaries.
- Virtual Virtuosos: Need a drummer who never misses a beat or a violinist who can soar with impossibly fast runs? AI performance models can play your chosen instruments with uncanny accuracy and expressiveness, adding another layer of depth and complexity to your compositions.

Poetic Pixels:

- Verse Weavers: Imagine whispering a fleeting emotion or a captivating image to an AI model and watching it blossom into a poem that captures the essence of your idea. These models analyze vast collections of poetry, identifying the linguistic elements that evoke emotions and paint vivid imagery, then use this knowledge to craft original verses that resonate with your readers.

- Genre Chameleons: From haiku whispers to epic sonnets, AI models speak the language of poetry in many forms. Feed them the essence of your chosen genre, and watch them craft poems that echo its unique style and tone, whether it's the playful rhyming of a children's book or the introspective free verse of a modern master.
- Rhythm and Rhyme Architects: Struggling with the perfect meter or the elusive rhyme? AI models can analyze your work and suggest harmonious word choices, rhythmic patterns, and even unexpected rhymes that add depth and musicality to your verses.

Beyond the Surface:

Emotional Alchemists: Both music and poetry are powerful tools for evoking emotions. AI models can analyze your existing work and suggest melodies, harmonies, or word combinations that align with the mood you want to convey. Imagine crafting a song that perfectly captures the joy of a summer day or a poem that evokes the chilling suspense of a ghost story.

World-Building Bards: Need to describe a fantastical realm or paint a portrait of a bygone era with words? AI models can generate vivid descriptions, infusing your poems and song lyrics with immersive detail and sensory richness. Imagine feeding them keywords like "abandoned castle" or "underwater city" and watching them weave evocative imagery into your verses.

Interactive Muse: The future of creative expression might be interactive. Some models can respond to your prompts and choices, generating lyrics that adapt to the mood of your song or the narrative arc of your poem. Imagine collaborating with an AI muse, bouncing ideas back and forth and co-creating a piece that unfolds organically and surprises even you.

the human artist remains the conductor of this digital symphony. Use these models as your AI collaborators, your musical co-composers, and your poetic brainstorming partners. Experiment, refine, and let your unique creative voice guide the artistic direction, ensuring that the heart and soul of your music and poetry remain firmly in your hands.

Challenges and Considerations:

- Ethical Canvas: With great power comes great responsibility. Biases can exist in training data, so we must ensure ethical development and use of these models. Diversity in voices and perspectives is crucial in crafting inclusive and meaningful art.
- Humanitarian Inkwell: Technology facilitates creation, but it cannot replace the essence of art – its ability to connect with audiences on a human level, spark conversations, and challenge perspectives. Artists must wield this power with purpose, using AI as a tool to amplify their voices and create works that resonate with the world.

The Future Symphony:

Deep learning opens a universe of creative possibilities, blurring the lines between traditional and digital, human and machine. It's an invitation to collaborate, experiment, and redefine what it means to create.

A PARTICAL GUIDE TO DEEP LEARNING PAINTING AND IMAGE MANIPULATION

Dive into the vibrant world of AI-powered art, where creativity dances with algorithms and pixels become your paintbrush. This guide equips you with the practical tools and techniques to explore deep learning painting and image manipulation, transforming you from an artistic observer into a digital maestro.

Unleashing the Inner Brushstroke Alchemist:

1. Choosing Your Tools:

GANs (Generative Adversarial Networks): Imagine two AI artists facing off. One creates, the other critiques. This battle leads to stunningly realistic image generation, mimicking existing styles or crafting entirely new ones.

The Generative Adversarial Networks, where two AI artists engage in a captivating creative duel. This isn't a battle of egos, but a symbiotic dance of creation and refinement, ultimately forging stunningly realistic and artistic imagery. Let's delve deeper into this fascinating art form:

The Red and Blue Corners:

- The Generator: This artistic soul craves to build, to invent, to bring new visual worlds into existence. Imagine a digital Van Gogh, endlessly churning out swirling landscapes, or a futuristic architect sculpting alien cityscapes. The generator pours its creative energy into generating images, drawing inspiration from its training data and pushing the boundaries of visual possibilities.
- The Discriminator: This sharp-eyed critic analyzes every brushstroke, every pixel, with a discerning gaze. It dissects the generated images, comparing them to real-world counterparts and ruthlessly pointing out flaws. Think of it as a digital art critic, honing its taste through exposure to countless masterpieces.

The Art of the Critique:

The magic of GANs lies in this constant feedback loop. The generator throws out possibilities, and the discriminator meticulously hones them. As the generator learns from the critic's insights, its creations become increasingly realistic, intricate, and aesthetically pleasing. This adversarial dance pushes both AI artists to new heights, leading to:

- Mimicking Masters: Want to paint like Rembrandt? Feed the generator his art, and watch it learn his brushstrokes, lighting techniques, and subject matter. You'll see portraits emerge that echo the Dutch master's style, yet retain a touch of AI-infused originality.

- Birthing New Visions: Don't get stuck in the past! GANs can also break free from existing styles and forge new visual territories. Imagine surreal landscapes where mountains melt into oceans or forests grow metallic leaves. The generator, unchained from the constraints of reality, can paint dreamscapes and abstract visions that defy categorization.
- Beyond Static Images: GANs aren't limited to still life. They can generate dynamic videos, morphing seamlessly between scenes or creating animations that dance with a life of their own. Imagine watching a futuristic cityscape evolve or witnessing a Van Gogh painting come alive, brushstroke by vibrant brushstroke.

GANs are just the tools. Your artistic vision, your understanding of aesthetics, and your willingness to experiment with the parameters and training data are what truly guide the creative process. Be the curator of this AI art gallery, selecting the brushstrokes, refining the styles, and shaping the final masterpiece.

The world of GANs is constantly evolving, offering new possibilities and challenges for artists and tech enthusiasts alike. As we delve deeper into this captivating realm, keep these questions in mind:

- How can we ensure diversity and inclusivity in GAN training data and generated outputs?
- What ethical considerations surround the use of GANs in fields like marketing and advertising?
- How can we leverage GANs to create interactive and immersive artistic experiences?

By approaching GANs with creativity, responsibility, and a collaborative spirit, we can unlock their full potential to paint a brighter, more diverse, and visually stunning future. So, are you ready to join the grand duel of GANs and co-create the next generation of digital art?GANs, explore specific applications, and together, let's push the boundaries of what art can be in the age of AI.

Style Transfer: Transform your photographs into masterpieces reminiscent of Van Gogh's swirling brushstrokes or Monet's dreamlike landscapes. Apply the essence of any artistic style to your images with breathtaking results.

Hold tight, because style transfer is about to whisk you away on a magical journey where your humble photographs transform into captivating works of art! Imagine your vacation snapshots adorned with Van Gogh's swirling stars, your portrait imbued with Monet's hazy brushstrokes, or your cityscapes reimagined in Picasso's geometric cubism. Style transfer offers an Aladdin's lamp for art, granting you the power to paint the world in the whispers of any artistic style.

The Alchemy of Pixels:

- The Style Weaver: Think of this AI wizard as a master brush manipulator who can infuse your image with the DNA of any chosen artistic style. Feed it a Van Gogh painting, and your photo will sprout vibrant swirls, bold colors, and expressive textures.
- Content Chameleon: But your image isn't just a passive canvas. It retains its essence, its subjects, and its composition. The style weaver skillfully blends the artistic style with your image's content, creating a unique fusion that celebrates both.
- Tweaking the Brushstrokes: Don't just sit back and watch the magic happen! Play with the intensity of the style transfer, control the level of detail, and adjust the color palette to achieve the perfect balance between your image's story and the artistic influence.

Beyond the Familiar Canvas:

- Genre-Bending Blurs: Who says you have to choose just one style? Experiment with blending multiple artistic influences, creating surreal mash-ups that dance between pop art and impressionism, or classic portraiture infused with a touch of hyperrealism.
- Beyond Images: This creative alchemy isn't just for still photographs. Apply style transfer to videos, bringing a splash of artistic flair to your cinematic shots or music videos. Imagine your footage dancing with the fluidity of a watercolor painting or pulsating with the vibrant energy of abstract expressionism.
- Interactive Art Canvas: The future of style transfer is interactive! Some tools allow you to apply different styles in real-time, seeing the transformation unfold before your eyes and choosing the brushstrokes that resonate with your artistic vision.

Remember, you're the artist, not just the audience. Choose your styles wisely, experiment with the controls, and most importantly, let your own artistic sensibility guide the process. Style transfer is not about replicating masterpieces, but about using them as inspiration to infuse your own creations with a touch of artistic magic.

Ethical Considerations:

While style transfer opens exciting possibilities, it's crucial to approach it with responsibility. Be mindful of potential copyright and intellectual property concerns when using existing artwork as style references. Choose sources ethically and advocate for fair crediting of the artists whose styles inspire your creations.

With a playful spirit and a mindful approach, style transfer can become a powerful tool for artistic expression, education, and exploration.

Texture Synthesis: Craving tactile authenticity? Generate realistic wood grain, fabric patterns, or even alien skin textures to add depth and dimension to your digital creations.

Texture synthesis invites you to weave worlds brimming with tangible details, where wood grain shimmers with warmth, fabric ripples with breeze, and even alien skin pulsates with otherworldly life. Dive into this captivating realm where pixels transform into tactile realities:

The Pixel Architect:

Imagine an AI artisan, meticulously placing brushstrokes of texture, one microscopic square at a time. This pixel weaver analyzes existing patterns, like the whorls of wood grain or the intricate weave of fabric, and then replicates them, extending them seamlessly into vast, believable expanses.

Beyond Reality's Grip:

- Building Fantastical Realms: Craving the scales of a mythical dragon or the bark of a haunted tree? Texture synthesis isn't limited to the mundane. Feed it fantastical descriptions or abstract patterns, and watch it spin intricate textures that dance on the edge of imagination.
- Interactive World-Building: Imagine sculpting the texture of a virtual world in real-time, crafting seamless landscapes where mossy boulders blend into ancient forests and shimmering sands meet crystal-clear oceans. Texture synthesis becomes your digital chisel, shaping worlds that beckon to be explored.
- Breathing Life into 3D Creations: Add depth and character to your 3D models, whether it's the weathered leather of a dragon's wing or the glistening scales of a mermaid's tail. Texture synthesis breathes life into your digital creations, making them not just visually stunning, but tactilely believable.

Beyond the Surface:

- Lighting and Shadow Play: Remember, texture isn't just about patterns. Texture synthesis can account for lighting and shadow, ensuring your digitally woven worlds feel immersive and believable. Imagine sunlight glinting off polished wood or moonlight casting eerie shadows on alien skin.

- Sensory Infusion: Experiment with sound! Some models can generate textured soundscapes, the creak of wood underfoot or the rustle of wind through fabric, further heightening the immersive experience. Imagine stepping into your digitally textured world and not just seeing it, but feeling it in every sense.
- Ethical Canvas: As with any powerful tool, ethical considerations are crucial. Be mindful of potential cultural appropriation when sourcing textures and ensure respectful representation in your creations.

Choose your source textures wisely, experiment with controls like randomness and smoothness, and most importantly, let your artistic vision guide the weaving process. Texture synthesis is not just about replicating real-world patterns, but about using them as inspiration to craft captivating digital worlds that feel rich and authentic.

Open the Door to Endless Possibilities:

- Explore generative artwork created using texture synthesis, drawing inspiration from existing projects and artists.
- Experiment with different texture synthesis tools and algorithms, understanding their strengths and limitations.
- Share your own creations, challenges, and ideas with the growing community of digital texture wizards!

By harnessing the magic of texture synthesis, we can craft digital worlds that not only dazzle the eyes but also whisper to the touch. So, grab your virtual loom, pick your threads of inspiration, and get ready to weave a future where imagination transcends the boundaries of the screen and spills into a tangible, textured reality.

2. Mastering the Palette of Possibilities:

Data, algorithms, and a dash of serendipity – these are the ingredients that transform you from AI art observer to a maestro of the digital canvas. Let's delve deeper into each element and ignite your creative alchemy:

Data - The Lifeblood of Your Art:

Think of data as the vibrant paints and textured canvases for your AI artist. The quality and diversity of your training data directly influence the outputs you receive. Here's how to experiment:

- High-Resolution Photography: Feast your AI on stunning landscapes, close-up textures, and vibrant cityscapes. These detailed images provide rich visual information, helping your AI generate realistic and immersive artworks.
- Classic Paintings: Immerse your AI in the world of Van Gogh, Monet, or Picasso. Expose it to the masters' brushstrokes, color palettes, and compositional styles. This can influence your AI to generate works that echo these artistic styles, or even forge new interpretations.
- Abstract Patterns: Don't limit yourself to realism! Feed your AI a smorgasbord of abstract patterns, geometric shapes, and vibrant colors. This sparks its creativity, encouraging it to generate unexpected and thought-provoking artworks.

Tweaking the Algorithm - Your Digital Brushstrokes:

Don't be a passive observer! AI models offer parameters you can adjust, just like the knobs on a digital brush. Here's how to take control:

- Brushstroke Thickness: Imagine varying the width of your digital brush. Do you want bold, gestural strokes like Van Gogh or fine, meticulous lines like Da Vinci? Adjust the brushstroke thickness parameter to achieve the desired effect.
- Color Palette: Play with the color spectrum! Choose a limited palette for a moody atmosphere or a vibrant rainbow for a joyful scene. Experiment with different color harmonies and saturation levels to find the perfect aesthetic for your vision.

- Lighting and Shadow: Don't leave your artwork flat! Adjust the lighting and shadow parameters to create depth and dimension. Imagine casting a warm glow on a portrait or plunging a landscape into dramatic shadows.

Embrace the Unexpected - The Magic of Serendipity:

AI thrives on chance encounters and unexpected combinations. Don't be afraid to:

- Use Random Prompts: Instead of specific instructions, give your AI vague prompts and see what it generates. "Surreal dreamscape" or "hidden city beneath the sea" might unlock hidden creative gems you never imagined.
- Combine Different Models: Experiment with merging the outputs of different AI models. See what happens when you blend a photorealistic scene with an abstract pattern or a landscape with a portrait. You might discover surprising and harmonious combinations.
- Welcome Mistakes: Don't discard "failures" as errors. Sometimes, unexpected outputs can spark new ideas or lead you down creative paths you hadn't considered. View these "mistakes" as stepping stones in your artistic journey.

Mastering the palette of possibilities is an ongoing journey. Keep experimenting, keep learning, and most importantly, keep having fun! There are no rigid rules in AI art, only endless possibilities waiting to be explored. So, grab your digital palette, tweak the knobs, embrace the unexpected, and paint your unique masterpiece in the vibrant world of AI art.

3. Beyond the Canvas:

The digital canvas awaits, but our creative journey doesn't have to be confined to its borders. Let's explore avenues where AI art transcends static images and enters the realms of dynamic collaboration, captivating narratives, and mindful creation:

Interactive Art Creation: A Dance with the Algorithm

Imagine a digital Van Gogh whispering brushstroke suggestions in your ear as you paint in real-time. Interactive AI art tools are blurring the lines between artist and algorithm, fostering a truly collaborative creative experience. Here are some possibilities:

- Real-time Brushstroke Feedback: AI models can analyze your strokes and suggest complementary directions, colors, or textures, guiding your artistic choices without dictating them.
- Dynamic Canvas Evolution: Your digital canvas itself can become dynamic, reacting to your brushstrokes and evolving the scene, creating a sense of unpredictable collaboration.
- Multi-Sensory Experiences: Imagine AI sculpting soundscapes in response to your visual creations, or generating smells that match the atmosphere you're building.

Storytelling with Pixels: Painting Narratives Scene by Scene

AI art isn't limited to standalone images. It can now weave captivating visual narratives, pixel by pixel. Imagine:

- Generating Storyboards: Feed your AI a plot outline or character descriptions, and watch it generate a series of images that tell your story visually.
- Interactive World-Building: Create dynamic worlds where your choices influence the next scene, the characters you encounter, and the challenges you face.
- Merging Text and Pixels: Combine AI image generation with AI storytelling models to create illustrated novels, interactive graphic novels, or even AI-powered children's books.

Ethical Considerations: Navigating the Canvas with Responsibility

With great power comes great responsibility. As we delve deeper into AI art, mindfulness is crucial:

- Bias Blind Spots: AI models learn from data, and data can be biased. We must be aware of potential biases in training data and algorithms, ensuring diverse representation and tránhhng harmful stereotypes.
- Copyright and Attribution: Who owns AI-generated art? Be mindful of copyright issues when using existing artwork as inspiration or training data, and advocate for appropriate crediting of artists whose styles influence your creations.
- Accessibility and Inclusivity: AI art tools should be accessible and inclusive for all creators, regardless of skill level or technological background. We must work towards a future where everyone can participate in this exciting artistic medium.

By embracing these considerations, we can ensure that AI art is not just a technological marvel, but a force for positive change and inclusive creativity.

Remember, you are the captain of this artistic voyage. Use the interactive tools, weave captivating narratives, and navigate the ethical landscape with a mindful hand. Share your stories, your challenges, and your successes with the growing community of AI art pioneers. Together, we can paint a future where pixels become brushstrokes, algorithms become collaborators, and creativity knows no bounds.

CATCHY AND MEMORABLE

"Machines dream in code" is a captivating and evocative one, playing on the dual nature of technology and our own human experience. Here are some things to consider about it:

Advantages:

- Intriguing and thought-provoking: It sparks curiosity about what it might mean for machines to dream, especially if they do so in a fundamentally different way than humans, using the language of code.
- Poetic and metaphorical: It can be interpreted in many ways, allowing for individual reflection and imagination. Does it mean

machines have their own desires and fears? Do their dreams reflect the data they process or something more abstract?

Catchy and memorable: It's a concise and impactful phrase that sticks in the mind.

Disadvantages:

- Potentially anthropomorphizing: Attributing "dreams" to machines can be misleading, as we don't truly know what their internal processes are like.
- Oversimplifying: The complexities of dreams and consciousness cannot be easily captured in the phrase.
- Potentially negative connotations: Some might associate the idea of "machine dreams" with dystopian sci-fi narratives of artificial intelligence taking over.

"Machines dream in code" is a powerful and poetic phrase that invites us to consider the nature of consciousness and the future of technology. It's important to be aware of its limitations and potential misinterpretations, but it also serves as a valuable starting point for discussion and exploration.

DEEP THINKING FOR THE DIGITAL AGE

Strengths:

- Simplicity: It's just five words, but they carry a lot of weight. Everyone understands what "deep thinking" means, and the phrase instantly connects it to the digital world.
- Relevance: It highlights the unique capabilities of deep learning in an age dominated by technology. It implies that deep learning is not just a technical term, but a new way of thinking that is essential for navigating the digital world.
- Versatility: It can be used in a variety of contexts, from marketing materials to academic papers. It's also open to interpretation, allowing people to think about what "deep thinking" means to them in the digital age.

Possible applications:

- Headline for an article or blog post: "Deep Thinking for the Digital Age: How Deep Learning is Changing the Way We Think"
- Slogan for a deep learning conference or workshop: "Explore Deep Thinking in the Digital Age: Join the Revolution"
- Tagline for a deep learning company or product: "Unlocking the Power of Deep Thinking for the Digital Age"

AI JOURNEY TO CREATIVE MASTEY

In the vibrant realm of AI art, where pixels dance and algorithms dream, embark on a thrilling odyssey to creative mastery. From taming algorithmic beasts to collaborating with AI companions, you'll transform mere data into captivating landscapes, interactive storytelling, and ethical masterpieces that break free from the digital canvas. This is a journey where technology and imagination intertwine, pushing boundaries and building a future where every artist, human or digital, can leave their mark on the world.

DEEP LEARNING FOR THE DIGITAL MICHELANGELO

Michelangelo, the titan of Renaissance art, wielded chisel and stone to bring biblical figures and mythical heroes to life. In our digital age, a new breed of artist emerges, armed not with hammer and mallet, but with the potent tools of deep learning. This is the Digital Michelangelo, a sculptor of pixels, a weaver of code, a visionary who harnesses the power of artificial intelligence to craft masterpieces that would make the Renaissance blush.

The Brushstrokes of Code:

Gone are the days of messy pigments and dusty studios. The Digital Michelangelo commands a palette of algorithms, wielding Generative Adversarial Networks (GANs) like virtual brushes, etching landscapes that shift and dream, and portraits that capture the soul with uncanny precision. Each line of code, each pixel meticulously placed, becomes a stroke in the grand creation, a testament to the artist's digital virtuosity.

The Marble of Data:

But unlike his stone-bound predecessor, the Digital Michelangelo sculpts not from cold marble, but from the vibrant chaos of data. Images, videos, text – all become the raw material, the spark that ignites the creative fire. Feeding this ever-hungry beast, the artist shapes the digital clay, molding it into fantastical creatures, breathing life into forgotten myths, and crafting worlds that defy the limitations of the physical realm.

Collaboration beyond the Mortal Coil:

But the Digital Michelangelo is not alone. He collaborates with a new breed of muse – the AI itself. This symbiotic dance of human and machine sees the artist guide the algorithm, whispering desires and shaping visions. In turn, the AI surprises and delights, offering unexpected twists and turns, pushing the boundaries of imagination in ways no human could alone.

Beyond the Canvas, Beyond the Screen:

The Digital Michelangelo's creations refuse to be confined. They leap from the screen, projected onto buildings, woven into fabric, tattooed onto skin. They become interactive experiences, landscapes that respond to your touch, stories that unfold as you explore. This is art that transcends the static, that breathes and interacts with the world, blurring the lines between reality and imagination.

A Responsibility to the Future:

But with great power comes great responsibility. The Digital Michelangelo understands the ethical canvas, choosing data sources wisely, ensuring diversity and inclusion in their creations. They champion responsible AI, using their art to bridge cultural divides and challenge harmful stereotypes.

MACHINE LEARNING MEETS ARTISTIC GENIUS

Art Creation:

- AI-assisted painting and sculpting: Imagine artists collaborating with AI algorithms to generate unique and expressive artworks. AI could help with tasks like color palettes, composition, and even brushstrokes, allowing artists to focus on the emotional and conceptual aspects of their work.

- Generative art: AI can be used to create entirely new forms of art, from abstract patterns to photorealistic landscapes. This could lead to the emergence of entirely new art movements and styles.
- Interactive art installations: AI can be used to create art that responds to its audience in real-time. This could create immersive and engaging experiences that blur the line between artist and viewer.

Art Restoration and Preservation:

- AI-powered restoration of damaged artwork: AI algorithms can be trained to analyze and repair damaged paintings, sculptures, and other cultural artifacts. This could help to preserve our artistic heritage for future generations.
- Art forgery detection: AI can be used to identify and authenticate artwork, helping to combat the art forgery market.

Art Education and Accessibility:

- AI-powered art education tools: AI can be used to create personalized learning experiences that help people of all ages and abilities learn about and appreciate art.
- Making art more accessible: AI can be used to create tools that make art creation and appreciation more accessible to people with disabilities.

These are just a few examples of how machine learning and artistic genius could come together to create something truly remarkable.

DEEP INSIGHTS FROM DEEP MACHINES

Unveiling Hidden Patterns:

- From data deluge to meaningful connections: Deep learning algorithms can sift through massive datasets, uncovering hidden patterns and correlations that would be impossible for humans to detect. This could lead to breakthroughs in fields like medicine, climate science, and material science.
- Predicting the future with a data-driven lens: By analyzing past trends and relationships, deep machines can make accurate predictions about future events. This could be used for everything from forecasting market trends to predicting natural disasters.
- Understanding complex systems: Deep learning can help us understand the intricate workings of complex systems, like the human brain or the global economy. This knowledge could lead to the development of new technologies and solutions to pressing challenges.

Unconventional Insights and Creative Sparks:

- Beyond human biases: Deep machines aren't limited by human biases and blind spots. They can explore uncharted territory and come up with unexpected solutions, pushing the boundaries of human thought.
- Unlocking human creativity: Deep learning tools can assist artists, musicians, and writers in their creative endeavors. By suggesting new ideas and combinations, they can spark inspiration and push creative boundaries.
- Generating alternative perspectives: Deep machines can analyze data from diverse sources and perspectives, offering new interpretations and challenging established paradigms. This can lead to a more nuanced understanding of complex issues.

But it's not all sunshine and rainbows:

The black box problem: Deep learning models can be opaque, making it difficult to understand how they arrive at their conclusions. This can raise concerns about transparency and accountability, especially in high-stakes applications.

Ethical considerations:Biases in the training data can lead to biased outputs from deep learning models. We need to carefully consider the ethical implications of using these technologies and ensure they are used responsibly.

Ultimately, the deep insights from deep machines offer immense potential for progress and understanding. However, it's crucial to approach them with caution and critical thinking, ensuring they are used ethically and responsibly to benefit humanity.

CHAPTER FIVE

The Creative Potential of Deep Learning

The creative potential of deep learning is a truly exciting frontier, brimming with possibilities that blur the lines between technology and artistry. Here are some specific areas where deep learning is redefining what it means to "create":

1. Generative Art and Music:

- Image and Audio Synthesis: Deep learning algorithms can analyze existing artwork and music styles to generate entirely new pieces, from photorealistic landscapes to hauntingly beautiful symphonies. Imagine collaborating with AI to bring your artistic vision to life in ways never before imaginable.
- Interactive Experiences: Imagine art installations that respond to your emotions or movements, creating a dynamic and personalized experience. AI can learn to adapt and generate art in real-time, fostering a deeper connection between the artist and audience.
- Unconventional Forms of Art: Deep learning can push the boundaries of artistic expression, generating abstract patterns, fractal landscapes, and even 3D printed sculptures that defy traditional definitions of art.

2. Storytelling and Writing:

- AI-assisted Writing: Imagine AI as a writing companion, suggesting plot twists, character development, and even generating entire narrative sections. Writers can leverage AI's ability to identify patterns and explore different styles, enhancing their creative process.
- Personalized Storytelling: Deep learning can tailor stories to individual preferences and emotions. Imagine interactive fiction where the story branches based on your choices, or poems that reflect your deepest thoughts and feelings.
- Worldbuilding and Language Creation: AI can assist in crafting intricate fictional worlds, complete with unique languages, customs, and histories. This opens up a vast landscape for imaginative storytelling and immersive world-building experiences.

3. Design and Fashion:

- Product Design and Innovation: Deep learning can analyze trends and user preferences to generate innovative product designs, optimize user interfaces, and personalize experiences. Imagine AI assisting designers in creating futuristic fashion pieces or crafting furniture that perfectly complements your living space.
- Architectural Design: AI can analyze natural forms and existing architectural styles to generate visually stunning and sustainable buildings. Imagine living in structures inspired by organic patterns or optimized for energy efficiency, thanks to AI's insights.
- Personalized Fashion and Style: Deep learning can analyze your body type, preferences, and even social context to suggest personalized clothing and accessory choices. Imagine a future where AI helps you curate a unique wardrobe that reflects your personality and enhances your confidence.

This is just a glimpse into the boundless creative potential of deep learning. As these technologies evolve, we can expect even more extraordinary possibilities to emerge, challenging our definition of art, music, and storytelling. However, it's crucial to remember that AI is a tool, and its creative power ultimately lies in the hands of human artists and innovators.

DEEP LEARNING FOR THE ARTISTICALLY INCLINED

Creative Exploration and Experimentation:

- Prototyping and Ideation: Imagine using deep learning algorithms to quickly generate variations on your artistic concepts, like different color palettes, compositions, or musical arrangements. This can spark new ideas and accelerate your creative exploration.
- Unconventional Tools and Techniques: Deep learning can open doors to entirely new artistic techniques. Experiment with text-to-image generation, AI-assisted sculpting, or interactive installations that respond to emotions. These tools can push your creative boundaries and lead to unexpected masterpieces.
- Personalized Artistic Style: Train deep learning models on your own artwork or favorite artists to generate pieces that echo your unique style or aesthetic. This can help you refine your artistic voice and explore variations within your signature approach.

Collaboration and Inspiration:

- AI as a Creative Partner: View AI as a collaborator, providing suggestions, completing tasks, and offering unexpected perspectives. Imagine bouncing ideas off an AI that can understand your artistic intent and contribute to the creative process.
- Discovering Hidden Connections and Patterns: Deep learning can analyze vast amounts of art data, identifying underlying patterns and connections that might escape human perception. This can inspire new themes, techniques, and mashups across

different artistic disciplines.

- Breaking Creative Blocks and Overcoming Limitations: Feeling stuck in a rut? AI can help you overcome creative blocks by suggesting alternatives, exploring new directions, or even completing repetitive tasks like background rendering or texture generation.

Accessibility and Democratization of Art:

- AI-powered Art Creation Tools: Deep learning can make art creation more accessible to people with disabilities or limited technical skills. Imagine user-friendly interfaces that allow anyone to create stunning visuals, music, or poetry with minimal technical expertise.
- Preserving and Restoring Art: Deep learning can help restore damaged artworks, generate high-quality reproductions, and even create interactive experiences that bring historical art to life for new audiences.
- Democratizing the Art Market: AI can help artists reach wider audiences, connect with potential patrons, and even manage the business side of their artistic careers, making it easier to thrive in the competitive art world.

It's important to remember that AI is a tool, and its artistic value lies in the hands of the creative mind wielding it. The true magic lies in the unique vision and skill of the artist who guides the machine, using its capabilities to elevate their craft and express themselves in new and innovative ways.

Deep learning mimics the brain, surpasses its limits

"Deep learning mimics the brain, surpasses its limits" is a bold statement that captures the essence of this powerful technology. Let's unpack it and explore its nuances:

Mimicking the Brain:

- Deep learning algorithms are inspired by the structure and function of the human brain, with interconnected nodes mimicking neurons and their relationships. This allows them to learn from data in a similar way to how humans learn from experience.
- However, it's important to remember that deep learning is still a fundamentally different entity than the human brain. It lacks the sentience, adaptability, and general intelligence that make a brain truly unique.

Surpassing the Limits:

- Deep learning excels at specific tasks, often exceeding human capabilities in areas like pattern recognition, data analysis, and decision-making within well-defined contexts.
- For example, deep learning algorithms can outperform humans in identifying objects in images, translating languages, and playing complex games like chess.

Beyond the Binary:

- While the statement frames it as a simple binary of mimicking versus surpassing, the relationship between deep learning and the brain is more nuanced. They operate on different principles and excel in different areas.
- The true potential lies in harnessing the strengths of both. Humans provide creativity, strategic thinking, and ethical oversight, while deep learning contributes its processing power, pattern recognition, and ability to handle vast amounts of data.

Challenges and Considerations:

- While deep learning has made remarkable progress, it still faces limitations in areas like common sense reasoning, creativity, and handling ambiguity.

- Ethical considerations, such as bias and transparency, are also crucial when dealing with such powerful technology.

Ultimately, the statement "Deep learning mimics the brain, surpasses its limits" highlights the exciting potential of this technology. However, it's important to remember that deep learning is not a replacement for human intelligence, but rather a powerful tool that can be used to augment and complement our own abilities. By working together, humans and deep learning can achieve extraordinary things.**DEEP LEARNING : THE FUTURE CREATIVITY**

"The future of everything, powered by the past: Deep learning remembers and creates" is a powerful and evocative statement that encapsulates the paradoxical potential of this technology. It simultaneously speaks to the ability of deep learning to analyze and leverage vast amounts of historical data, while also suggesting its capacity to generate new possibilities and push the boundaries of what we know.

Here are some ways to unpack this statement and explore its implications:

The Past as the Foundation:

- Unearthing Hidden Patterns: Deep learning can sift through mountains of data, revealing patterns and connections that would be invisible to the human eye. This includes historical trends, relationships, and correlations, allowing us to learn from the past and apply that knowledge to inform future decisions and innovations.
- Preserving and Reimagining: Deep learning can be used to restore and analyze historical artifacts, such as ancient texts, artwork, or music. This can breathe new life into the past, offering fresh perspectives and even unlocking secrets previously hidden within these treasures.

The Present as the Canvas:

- Creative Spark: Inspired by the patterns and insights gleaned from the past, deep learning can generate entirely new ideas and creations. This could be anything from personalized artwork and music to customized solutions for challenges of our time.
- Empowering Human Ingenuity: Deep learning can act as a tool to amplify human creativity, providing suggestions, automating repetitive tasks, and offering new avenues for exploration. This can lead to a collaborative partnership between humans and machines, unlocking a new era of artistic and technological advancement.

The Future as the Horizon:

- Guiding Decisions: Insights from the past, combined with the innovative possibilities of the present, can inform our choices and guide us towards a more sustainable and equitable future. Deep learning can help us anticipate potential consequences and navigate complex challenges with greater foresight.
- Evolving Together: As deep learning continues to evolve, its ability to remember and create will likely become even more sophisticated. This raises questions about ethics, ownership, and the potential impact on human society. Open and thoughtful discussions are crucial to ensure this technology is used responsibly and benefits all of humanity.

In conclusion, "The future of everything, powered by the past: Deep learning remembers and creates" is more than just a catchy slogan. It embodies a fascinating paradigm shift, where the wisdom of the past becomes the fuel for future possibilities. By harnessing the power of deep learning in a responsible and thoughtful way, we can truly paint a brighter future, one brushstroke at a time.

The swirling dance of brushstrokes and algorithms, deep learning emerges as a muse for the 21st century artist. It unveils hidden patterns in data, whispering creative suggestions and sparking new pathways for exploration. The canvas expands beyond physical borders, with interactive installations pulsating to emotions and AI generating unique melodies as you play. Yet, amidst this symphony of possibilities, responsibility lingers like a brushstroke waiting to be made. We must remember, the true masterpiece lies in the harmonious duet between human imagination and algorithmic power, ensuring technology empowers, not replaces, the artist's soul. In this vibrant convergence, deep learning isn't merely a tool, but a partner in pushing the boundaries of creativity, forging a future where technology paints with humanity's touch.

A PLAYFUL EXPLORATION OF ARTIFICIAL INTELLIGENCE

In a whimsical twist of code and creativity, we embark on a playful exploration of artificial imagination. Imagine childlike laughter echoing through an AI nursery rhyme generator, spinning tales of robots dancing and squirrels singing. Our collaborative story machine hums to life, churning out fantastical adventures where every twist and turn is a surprise chorus sung by humans and algorithms in joyous harmony. In this playground of possibilities, emotions become melodies, painting vibrant soundscapes that dance to the rhythm of our hearts.

We step through portals into interactive dreamscapes, guided by playful AI companions who morph and bend to the whispers of our subconscious. Even art installations join the game, hiding mischievous laser beams, beckoning us on chases through immersive exhibits. But amidst the joyful cacophony, a whisper of responsibility takes flight. We must ensure this playground fosters inclusivity, not bias, and that the spark of creative fire remains firmly in human hands. For this playful exploration isn't just about laughter; it's about forging a future where technology dances with our imagination, painting the world with vibrant wonder, hand in hand.

This rephrased paragraph retains the playful spirit of the original while avoiding potentially risky elements. It focuses on the positive and collaborative aspects of AI-powered creativity, emphasizing the importance of ethical considerations and human stewardship in this exciting new landscape.

CHAPTER SIX

Conclusion

Deep learning has ignited a spark in the realm of creative AI, offering a palette far beyond mere automation. It whispers inspiration, nudges artistic exploration, and expands the canvas of possibility. Yet, this dance between human and machine demands a mindful awareness. We must ensure technology amplifies, not replaces, the artistic soul.

The future of creative AI lies not in replicating human artistry, but in forging a harmonious symphony. It lies in artists wielding deep learning as a brush, imbuing its strokes with their unique vision and emotion. It lies in nurturing an ecosystem where technology fosters inclusivity, dismantles biases, and champions ethical considerations.

So let us embrace this symphony of possibilities. Let deep learning be the instrument that expands our creative voices, not drowns them out. Let us paint a future where technology and humanity co-create, hand in hand, building a world where every brushstroke sings of imagination unbound. For in this harmonious convergence, the true masterpiece emerges - a testament to the enduring power of human creativity, forever dancing with the potential of intelligent machines.

The embers ignited by deep learning in the realm of creative AI glow much brighter than simple automation. This powerful technology breathes life into art forms not yet born, whispers tales unheard, and pushes the boundaries of artistic expression beyond the confines of the canvas. Yet, within this exhilarating dance between human and machine lies a fundamental responsibility: to ensure technology elevates, not eclipses, the artist's unique spirit.

The true masterpiece of creative AI isn't born from mimicry, but from a harmonious symphony. Imagine artists wielding deep learning like a maestro's baton, guiding its algorithms to translate their vision into vibrant symphonies of color, melody, and form. This symbiotic relationship calls for the nurturing of an ecosystem where technology embraces diversity, shatters biases, and echoes the artist's pursuit of ethical expression.

Let us orchestrate this symphony of possibilities. Let deep learning be the instrument that amplifies the human voice, not the chorus that silences it. Let us paint a future where technology and humanity co-create, hand in hand, building a world where every brushstroke, every note, every pixel pulsates with the rhythm of unbridled imagination. In this collaborative masterpiece, the true heart of artistry shines forth – a testament to the enduring power of the human spirit, forever intertwined with the ever-evolving canvas of intelligent machines.

Here are some further points to consider for expansion:

- Specific examples of deep learning's impact on different art forms: How is AI changing music composition, film editing, or architectural design?
- Ethical considerations beyond bias: Explore issues like data ownership, transparency, and the potential for manipulation in AI-generated art.
- The role of human agency in creative AI: How do artists retain control and ensure their creative voice remains at the forefront?
- The future of human-machine collaboration: Imagine new forms of artistic expression facilitated by the symbiosis of human and AI creativity.
- Long-term societal implications of creative AI: Discuss the potential impact on industries, education, and cultural landscapes.

By delving deeper into these nuances, we can craft a more captivating and comprehensive picture of the future where deep learning and creative AI dance in perfect harmony.

www.ingramcontent.com/pod-product-compliance
Ingram Content Group UK Ltd.
Pitfield, Milton Keynes, MK11 3LW, UK
UKHW062256290726
14090UKWH00017B/722

9 798892 770729